Before You Send Them Out: Countering a Culture of Unprepared Disciples

A New Church Member's Training Manual

Dr. Oscar T. Moses

sermontobook
.com

Sermon To Book
www.sermontobook.com

Before You Send Them Out / Oscar T. Moses
ISBN-13: 9780692688854
ISBN-10: 0692688854

Dedication

Before You Send Them Out is dedicated to the sainted memory of my maternal grandparents, Reverend Joseph A. Allen and Dorothy Webb Allen, and paternal grandparents, O. T. Moses and Bobbie Lou Moses, for their spiritual investments.

Additionally, this work is dedicated to my parents, the late Deacon Oscar Moses and Rosetta Moses-Hill, for providing unconditional love and a strong Christian foundation that has anchored the faith tenets within the writer's heart. This work is dedicated to the late R. Lillian Gladney for her unselfish love and sacrificial living.

This work is further dedicated to the writer's brother and sister, David Allen Moses and Kelly Ann Moses, for their loving and prayerful support throughout the entire process. It is also dedicated to the writer's young niece and nephew, Taylor Vaughn Moses and David Andrew Moses, and young cousin, Roderiqua Williams. It is for these young persons that the writer prays to leave as a legacy the importance of furthering one's education.

Finally, this work is lovingly and eternally dedicated to my wife, Dr. Jacqueline M. Moses, for her indomitable spirit and her faith in God and the writer's ability to complete this project.

Acknowledgements

Sincere appreciation, love, and respect are given to my wife, Dr. Jacqueline Marie Moses, for providing loving support, honest feedback, and ongoing encouragement.

Heartfelt appreciation to the writer's parents, Rosetta Moses Hill and the late Oscar Moses, for providing a model of discipleship and a Christian home. The writer expresses great appreciation to his only sibling, David A. Moses, his wife Kelly, and their two children, Taylor V. Moses and David Andrew Moses, for providing ongoing loving support. Loving appreciation to Pastor William R. Lott and First Lady Chris Lott for their spiritual and prayerful support.

Special appreciation and gratitude goes to the entire membership of The Mount Hermon Missionary Baptist Church and the Illinois National Baptist Convention under the leadership of Dr. Joel D. Taylor for their patience and willingness to participate in the process to develop this model of ministry.

Finally, above all, praise to God for His Sovereign Existence, Love, Promises, Providence, and Challenge to the Church.

CONTENTS

Abstract

Before You Send Them Out is designed to assist congregations in equipping members to do the work of evangelism effectively and avoid the cycle of developing insecure disciples, damaging doctrine, and diminishing witnessing power. The reader will discover the biblical history of preparing disciples to do the work of evangelism and modern approaches to evangelism. *Before You Send Them Out* will present a teaching ministry model by providing an outline of five (5) classes that will teach the reader basic biblical knowledge as a prerequisite to evangelistic ministry. Finally, this book will give conclusions and a summary as it relates to preparing church members to evangelize by applying this model.

INTRODUCTION

We Have a Responsibility to Make Disciples

In Mark 8:27, Jesus asked His followers, "Who do men say that I am?" (NKJV). Surprisingly, His closest followers responded incorrectly, with the exception of Peter. This biblical account confirms that even those who physically walked closely with Jesus had a difficult time answering this question. However, over time and through teaching, they became conscious of who Jesus was and were most effective in carrying out His mandate to their generation.

The Book of Acts details the historical account of the early church growing enormously because Christians were able to articulate their belief in Jesus Christ, and their mandate to expand His Church. On the Day of Pentecost, Peter preached the *Word of God*. As a result, "they that gladly received his word were baptized: and the same day there were added unto them about three thousand souls" (Acts 2:41 KJV).

The growth of the early church did not happen on preaching alone. Acts 2:42 says, "And they continued steadfastly in the apostles' doctrine and fellowship, and in breaking of bread, and in prayers" (NKJV). In other words, early Christians continued to study God's Word to become equipped to carry out the mandate that Jesus left to "grow" the church.

Two thousand years later, most Christians cannot answer the question that Jesus posed to His followers in Mark 8:27, "Who do men say that I am?" (NKJV). The many different answers to this question have created a distorted picture of the historical Jesus Christ. Ask the modern Christian whom Jesus is and you are sure to get several different answers that contrast with the Jesus of Scripture. The result is a culture that has shifted the movement of the church from the *progressive* church in Acts 2 to the *regressive* church of 2015.

No wonder people are leaving the church. Most Christians cannot explain who Jesus is. Although many confess their love for Christ, they could not begin to tell you why, even though 1 Peter 3:15 exhorts the Christian to "be ready always to give an answer" (KJV).

This has created a problem. Souls cannot be won for Christ if Christians can't explain who He is and what He stands for. If the business of the church is to win souls, statistically we are not doing a good job. Katherine T. Phan, a Christian reporter, cited a quote by the Barna Group that 31 million people have been a part of an "exodus from the church."[1] David Sanford further suggested that many are leaving the church because no one discusses difficult biblical issues. Sanford said, "Any business that is losing 31 million customers is going out of business."[2]

In an article titled "Most Christians Cannot Explain Their Faith," Christian correspondent Edmond Chua gave findings by the Barna Group that only 9 percent of Americans believe that the Bible is totally accurate in its teachings and principles.[3] In other words, those outside of the 9 percent pick and choose what they want to believe. Who wants to join a movement when no one can explain what the movement is about? Jesus told us to make disciples, and that cannot happen until we know whom Jesus is, what He told us to do, and how He told us to do it.

The practice of teaching God's words to disciples has been lost in a wave of relativism, existentialism, and pragmatism. The result is a growing surface of non-biblical Christians that do not embrace historical biblical truth, and an exodus of Christians that are void of biblical answers. As a result, the church has experienced diminishing witnessing power, damaged doctrine, and the development of insecure disciples. The effect of *not knowing whom Jesus is* has placed the Church of Jesus Christ in a crisis, with people leaving in great numbers.

CHAPTER ONE

Where Are the Disciples of Christ?

In gathering data about trends for making disciples, several pieces of literature were reviewed to construct a foundation for the five-part lesson plan. This chapter will observe the consensus of authors, pastors, researchers, and scholars who have weighed in on the church and discipleship in the twenty-first century.

Why Aren't We Sharing the Gospel?

I stumbled across a blog post by Tim McKnight that gave "Five Reasons We Don't Make Disciples."[4]

We Fail to Love God and People

McKnight observes that we are not loving God according to John 14:15: "If you love me, you will keep my commandments" (ESV). We also don't love people as we are called to do. We should be moved by Christ's love to share the gospel as His ambassadors (see 2 Corinthians 5:11-20).

We Don't Believe Christ Is the Only Way

McKnight further notes that not all Christians "think sharing the gospel is essential for salvation."

> *A recent poll states that 92 percent of evangelicals believe that people are saved only through Jesus Christ; however, another survey of Protestant church attenders indicates that 48 percent of Protestants believe that people can obtain eternal life by sincerely following other religions apart from Christianity.*

If we really believe that the only way to be saved is through hearing the gospel of Christ and believing, then we will share the gospel and make disciples.

We Are Afraid

We may fear embarrassment or rejection at the hands of people who do not understand and believe the gospel. We may fear alienating people we care about and damaging relationships.

Jesus said, "And behold, I am with you always, to the end of the age" (Matthew 28:20 ESV). We don't need to be afraid. Christ is with us to strengthen, encourage, and comfort us. The Holy Spirit will empower our sharing of the Good News and the word of God if we step out in faith (see Acts 4:31).

We Don't Feel Prepared

We may shrink from sharing the gospel because we do not feel we have the knowledge or skill to do it properly. As Christians, we are called to tell people about our Savior, Jesus, and how He works in our lives (see Acts 1:8). It is our responsibility to know Scripture and understand the basics of our faith as found in God's word so we can effectively communicate them to other people. We need to study the Bible regularly so we are prepared to make disciples.

All Scripture is breathed out by God and profitable for teaching, for reproof, for correction, and for training in righteousness, that the man of God may be complete, equipped for every good work. — 2 Timothy 3:16-17 (ESV)

The Church Is on Life Support

James MacDonald's *Vertical Church* has a chapter called the "Unafraid Witness." MacDonald states, "Some suggest that boldness is a matter of personality or preference, not binding on all Christians at all times. Paul, however, clarified that boldness isn't just a good way; it's the right way, the God way, the biblical method for talking to people about Jesus."[5]

A book titled *Real Life Discipleship Training Manual* by Jim Putman and Avery T. Ellis emphasizes the need for those who are Christian to express their faith to the unchurched. They note that "in his book *The Unchurched Next Door*, Tom Rainer cites a study that most unchurched people do not sense that Christians actively try to share their faith and that many wonder what makes Christianity hesitant."[6]

Francis Chan says in his book *Multiply*, "We have developed a culture where the minister ministers and the rest of us sit back and enjoy church from a comfortable distance. This is not what God intends for His church. Every Christian is called by God to minister. You are called to make disciples."[7]

Just as baptism is more significant than we might have thought, so teaching people to obey Jesus' commands is an enormous task. Realistically, this will require a lifetime of devotion, studying the scriptures, and investing in the people around us.[8] Francis Chan makes this very compelling statement: "The members of the early church took their responsibility to make disciples very seriously. To them the church was not a corporation to be run by a CEO, rather they compared the church to a body that functioned properly when [each] member is doing its part."[9]

In 2007, the Barna Group reported an increase among atheists and agnostics, particularly among young people in America.[10]

According to a 2012 Pew study, "The number of Americans who do not identify with any religion continues to grow at a rapid pace. One-fifth of the U.S. public—and a third of adults under thirty—are religiously unaffiliated today, the highest percentages ever in Pew Research Center polling. Some of the religiously unaffiliated are spiritual or religious in some way; 30 percent believe with absolute certainty in a 'God or universal spirit,' 38 percent believe with less certainty. Twenty-one percent pray every day. Only 12 percent are atheist, and 17 percent are agnostic."[11]

However, there is a new group on the rise called *ignostics* that differs from the aforementioned. Both atheists and agnostics are familiar with conversations about God, but ignostics have no clue who God is:

> *The term "ignosticism" is a play on the words "ignorance" and "gnosticism." A direct meaning of ignosticism would mean something like, "ignorance of god(s)," meaning the ignostic doesn't know anything about gods, or doesn't know what the term "god" means. Typically, the ignostic takes a position of refraining from making arguments for or against the existence of god(s) until a coherent definition of "god" is provided. Many ignostics are also theological noncognitivists, although the two positions are not mutually inclusive.[12]*

Sherry Weddell makes a contribution to these alarming statistics in her book *Forming Intentional Disciples*: "Some 11.6 million Christians left Christianity in 2010. Add the number who chose to leave to the number of those converted, and we see an amazing number of people—roughly 27.6 million—moved deliberately out of the Christian world in a single year."[13]

The Church of Jesus Christ appears to be failing in the Great Commission to tell the world about the good news of salvation through Jesus Christ.

Currently there are 1.7 billion people with no access to the Good News of Jesus Christ. Approximately seventeen million people die every year without having heard the name of Jesus. One would argue that those statistics may suit third world countries, but sadly those numbers include people within the United States. George Barna states, "Today approximately 262 million people live in the United States. By my calculations, based on large scale surveys of the population, 187 million of those people have yet to accept Jesus Christ as their Lord and Savior."[14]

To add to the despondency, many people are leaving or never entering churches because of a lack of or no connection to biblical teaching or to God. Church membership is on the decline and churches are closing because they do not have members to sustain the ministry. The Church is on life support! Here are some of the reasons why:

- **A Rejection of the Traditional Church:** Many believe that the traditional church is outdated. Church does not relate to the time of this generation.
- **The Rise of Pluralism:** Pluralism says that all roads lead to God and that church denomination or membership is not necessary. Pluralism is one of the fastest-growing belief systems in the country. It is also called *inclusive theology*. Pluralism (or inclusive theology) is gaining rapid ground in churches and seminaries around the world.

- **Upcoming Millennials:** Millennials are swiftly coming to the front today. Millennials tend to be more self-absorbed. They prefer progressing with career versus progressing with God. Church is an option for Millennials whereas it was a priority for previous generations. As a consequence, numbers are down in many churches around the country.
- **The Negative Stigma:** Some people think that all churches and preachers are out for money.
- **Church Hypocrisy:** "The pastor was in the club with me last night."
- **Television Pastors:** This is the "Joel Olsteen or T.D. Jakes is my pastor" generation. Although televangelism has led many to Jesus Christ, it has also allowed many to feel that they are excused from the responsibility of church membership.
- **Religion versus Relationship:** Some feel as though they do not want to be connected to a specific denomination. There are many who want to break away from denominationalism because of their experiences growing up with stringent rules in the church.
- **Conformity:** We have lowered the standard for churches trying to reach the world.
- **Boredom:** Many young people do not want anything to do with the church. They feel that it is a boring place to be.

- **Unequipped Christians:** Many people that attend churches cannot articulate the basic essentials of the faith.

Dr. Randy Douglass is an adjunct professor of religion at Charleston Southern University and a Bible teacher at Palmetto Christian Academy in Mount Pleasant, SC. He is a very strong proponent for training as a means to prepare new members for evangelism and becoming vital components of the church.

He makes a profound argument as to why the church is in decline. Douglass's research has revealed the need for educating converts in the basic essentials of the Christian faith. In an October 21, 2009 article titled "Closing the Back Door: The Need for Christian Education," Douglass stresses the point that what lies beneath the surface of young people abandoning the church is a lack of understanding and mistrust of the Bible. He states that the "back door is open," meaning that many young people have left the church.[15]

Douglass found the reasons young adults gave for abandoning the church fell into five general categories. Five of the most common reasons include: "life-change issues" (97 percent), "I wanted a break from church" (27 percent), "I moved to college and stopped attending church" (25 percent), "work responsibilities prevented me from attending" (23 percent), and "I moved too far away from church to continue attending" (22 percent).[16]

Digging deeper into what seemed like surface issues, Douglass discovered an underlying current that led to church abandonment by the upcoming generation.

Beemer discovered that biblical disbelief was at the root of the departure of many young people, and provided several solutions to counter this problem. He had assumed that Sunday school, or some teaching arm of the church, had been implemented in the church they attended. Although many had attended church training, many of them had not been properly instructed on basic biblical principles and had very little knowledge of the faith. Beemer concluded that effective discipleship must address these doubts in the hearts about Scripture.[17]

> *Come unto me, all ye that labour and are heavy laden, and I will give you rest. Take my yoke upon you, and learn of me; for I am meek and lowly in heart: and ye shall find rest unto your souls. For my yoke is easy, and my burden is light.* — *Matthew 11:28–30 (KJV)*

WORKBOOK

Chapter 1 Questions

Question: Do you agree that many people who attend churches cannot articulate the basic essentials of the faith? Why or why not? How well can you share the basics?

_____

_____

_____

_____

_____

_____

_____

_____

_____

_____

_____

Question: How has the current church failed to take seriously the responsibility to make disciples? Have you taken this responsibility seriously? Explain.

_____

_____

_____

_____

_____

_____

_____

_____

_____

_____

_____

Question: Do you agree that boldness is the biblical method for talking to people about Jesus? Why or why not? How often do you end up sharing your faith?

_____

_____

_____

_____

_____

_____

_____

_____

_____

_____

_____

Action: Every Christian is called by God to minister. The church of Jesus Christ appears to be failing in the Great Commission to tell the world about the good news of salvation through Jesus Christ. Biblical unbelief is at the root of the departure of many young people from the church. Effective discipleship must address doubts in the heart about Scripture. The Holy Spirit will empower our sharing of the Good News and the word of God if we step out in faith.

Chapter 1 Notes

_____

_____

_____

_____

_____

_____

_____

_____

_____

_____

_____

_____

_____

_____

_____

_____

_____

_____

_____

_____

_____

_____

_____

_____

CHAPTER TWO

Preparing Christians for Effective Evangelism

This training is designed to give basic biblical information to equip pastors to prepare congregations for effective evangelism.

In *The Equipping Pastor*, R. Paul Stevens and Phil Collins argue:

> *The hire and fire mentality of the North American society has reduced the pastor's ministry to a buy and sell commodity. A pastor with a vision to equip all the members for ministry, as proposed in Ephesians 4:11-12, is apt to run into the mentality, "We hired you to do ministry." Quaker Elton Trueblood gave his life to promoting the radical idea that pastors are not called to get people to assist them with their ministry; rather, the pastor is called to assist the people, the laity with their ministry both in the church and in the world. It will take a gracious conspiracy between pastor and people to bring this change about.*[18]

The purpose of this book is to engage pastors in the biblical process of making disciples through a simple process of teaching five biblical principles before engaging members in the process of evangelism and discipleship.

The Problem

Most confessing Christians cannot answer basic questions about their faith. Jude, the writer of the chapter that precedes Revelation, wrote to people who were called and loved by God to contend for the faith. We often ignore the book of Jude, but within its contents is a very practical message for the times in which we live. In verse 3 of the one-chapter book, Jude exhorts Christians to "contend for the faith" (KJV), to defend the faith they have embraced. This can be difficult if the contender knows not what he or she is contending. It's like an attorney trying to defend a case without knowing anything about it.

One reason many Christians are fearful and avoid conversation with other religions like the Jehovah Witnesses is because many are unsure about their faith.

The church is dying because of diminishing witnessing power, insecure disciples, and damaged doctrine.

Diminishing Witnessing Power

Christians cannot effectively witness with power if they are unsure of the power they have to witness. Acts

1:8 informs the Christian of unseen power to witness to the world, bearing the testimony of Jesus Christ. It is important to realize that God has promised power: not to climb the corporate ladder of success, but to witness. Just imagine how the church has diminished because of inaccurate interpretations of Jesus Christ. Culture has diminished the Christ of Scripture, and Christians have reduced their presentation of the gospel to become less offensive.

Insecure Disciples

When new converts come to Christ without accurate biblical knowledge of the Scriptures, they become insecure disciples, unsure of what they believe. This repeated behavior over time will generate a culture of insecure disciples that will represent the new normal.

Damaged Doctrine

Damaged doctrine evolves as a consequence of false teachers spreading erroneous teachings about Jesus Christ. Paul wrote to Timothy and reminded him to be insistent on teaching the true doctrine that he had learned to study diligently.

> *Of these things put them in remembrance, charging them before the Lord that they strive not about words to no profit, but to the subverting of the hearers. Study to shew thyself approved unto God, a workman that needeth not to be ashamed, rightly dividing the word of truth. — 2 Timothy 2:14-15 (KJV)*

If the church would recognize how the problems of diminishing witnessing power, insecure disciples, and damaged doctrine affect the members' ability to reach people effectively, then they could train and equip Christians to make an impact on current and future generations. Part of that process involves determining the purpose of the church and then learning how to live out that purpose.

Essentials for Effective Evangelism

In many ways, a church is like a business. A church needs to apply sound business principles and training in order to accomplish its purpose.

- What successful company would send a representative out without knowledge of the company business?
- Why does the church send representatives out with no knowledge of Kingdom Business?
- Why do we spend so little time training?
- How do we revive evangelism in the church?

The mission of the church is to win souls. However, 95 percent of Christians never win a soul to Christ. This training will address five basic tenets that the Christian worker of evangelism should understand when sharing the Good News. Not every church member is a disciple, yet the church should make available the basic essentials to prepare its membership to do the work of evangelism.

Not everyone will embrace the work of evangelism, but for those who are committed, this manual has five basic tenets designed as lessons that consist of basic biblical principles of preparation, which will lead to effective evangelism:

- **Saved Solid:** Before one can effectively do the work of evangelism, he or she must be able to answer the basic questions pertaining to salvation.
- **Soul Maintenance Plan:** The effective worker of evangelism should have a maturing and developing relationship with Jesus Christ.
- **Spiritual Gifts:** God has given every believer a gift. The effective worker of evangelism must use his or her God-given gifts.
- **Sowing Seeds of Salvation:** The effective worker of evangelism must know that there are various approaches.
- **Stewardship:** The effective worker of evangelism must understand that God holds him or her accountable to "use what you've got" to get the work of evangelism done.

WORKBOOK

Chapter 2 Questions

Question: Which of the three problems—diminishing witnessing power, insecure disciples, and damaged doctrine—most resonates with you? Why?

_____

_____

_____

_____

_____

_____

_____

_____

_____

_____

_____

Question: Have you at times fallen into the mindset that hired church leaders are the ones who should be doing ministry? Why or why not?

_____

_____

_____

_____

_____

_____

_____

_____

_____

_____

Question: Why is training church members in the gospel and evangelism important?

_____

_____

_____

_____

_____

_____

_____

_____

_____

_____

Action: If the church would recognize how the problems of diminishing witnessing power, insecure disciples, and damaged doctrine affect the members' ability to reach people effectively, then they could train and equip Christians to make an impact on current and future generations.

Chapter 2 Notes

_____

_____

_____

_____

_____

_____

_____

_____

_____

_____

_____

_____

_____

_____

_____

_____

_____

_____

_____

_____

_____

_____

_____

_____

CHAPTER THREE

A Biblical Foundation

How has the church biblically equipped Christians to do the work of evangelism? The best reference that informs the church of practices that prepared new converts to do the work of evangelism is the Holy Bible.

*My people are destroyed for lack of knowledge: because thou hast rejected knowledge, I will also reject thee, that thou shalt be no priest to me: seeing thou hast forgotten the law of thy God, I will also forget thy children. — **Hosea 4:6 (KJV)***

*Therefore my people are gone into captivity, because they have no knowledge: and their honourable men are famished, and their multitude dried up with thirst. — **Isaiah 5:13 (KJV)***

Knowledge of God has never been relaxed for those who follow Him. God has always required His people to know who He is and what His will and word for our lives are. God has promised blessings for those who know of Him.

> *Blessed is the man that walketh not in the counsel of the ungodly, nor standeth in the way of sinners, nor sitteth in the seat of the scornful. But his delight is in the law of the LORD; and in his law doth he meditate day and night. —* ***Psalm 1:1-2 (KJV)***

The Old Testament is loaded with scriptures (including the Ten Commandments) that require the people of God to have knowledge of who He is and what He requires. This theme carries into the New Testament. Jesus said, "Take my yoke upon you, and learn of me; for I am meek and lowly in heart: and ye shall find rest unto your souls" (Matthew 11:29 KJV). This theme continued during the ministry of Jesus. He taught His disciples daily. Therefore, that negates the need to defect from rigorous teaching in today's church.

After the death, burial, and resurrection of Jesus Christ, His followers were given specific instructions that would ultimately prepare them to carry out the work of evangelism. In Luke chapter 24, Jesus appeared to His terrified followers after the resurrection. The disciples were hiding in closed quarters, fearing for their lives. They were under the notion that they would be killed just as Jesus was.

Their faith in His words was not strong. They were insecure, paranoid, and in an indeterminate state of decision-making about their future as Disciples of Christ.

When Jesus appeared before them, they assumed that He was a ghost. Jesus ultimately proved to them that He was in fact alive and in human flesh.

> *Behold my hands and my feet, that it is I myself: handle me, and see; for a spirit hath not flesh and bones, as ye see me have. And when he had thus spoken, he shewed them his hands and his feet.* — **Luke 24:39–40 (KJV)**

Jesus knew that they were not able to carry out the work in their present state. He waited until they were equipped and empowered by the Holy Spirit.

> *And [Jesus] said unto them, Thus it is written, and thus it behooved Christ to suffer, and to rise from the dead the third day: And that repentance and remission of sins should be preached in his name among all nations, beginning at Jerusalem. And ye are witnesses of these things. And, behold, I send the promise of my Father upon you: but tarry ye in the city of Jerusalem, until ye be endued with power from on high.* — **Luke 24:46–49 (KJV)**

Jesus informed His followers of the task that lay before them to be witnesses and instructed them to go to Jerusalem and wait until they were filled with power from the Holy Spirit. In Acts 1:8, Luke records the words of Jesus: "But ye shall receive power, after that the Holy Ghost is come upon you: and ye shall be witnesses unto me both in Jerusalem, and in all Judaea, and in Samaria, and unto the uttermost part of the earth"

(KJV). Jesus informed the disciples that they would receive power to witness throughout the world.

The promise of receiving the Holy Spirit was confirmed on the day of Pentecost.

> *And when the day of Pentecost was fully come, they were all with one accord in one place. And suddenly there came a sound from heaven as of a rushing mighty wind, and it filled all the house where they were sitting. And there appeared unto them cloven tongues like as of fire, and it sat upon each of them. And they were all filled with the Holy Ghost, and began to speak with other tongues, as the Spirit gave them utterance. — Acts 2:1–4 (KJV)*

The Pentecostal experience in Jerusalem culminated the promise that Jesus assured His believers they would encounter before they were able to continue the work He had for them to accomplish.

After the Pentecostal experience, the once-timid followers of Jesus who appeared to be defectors of the cross became the forerunners of the cross. They took the initiative to create an atmosphere among believers that would equip and empower them to carry out the work of evangelism.

Evangelism, biblically ascribed in the context of the New Testament church, pertained to followers of Jesus Christ who embraced a lifestyle that led to opportunities to share the gospel, or "good news," of salvation through Jesus Christ. However, it is evident in the Acts of the Holy Spirit that new converts were trained before they were deployed to serve. Thousands of converts were baptized as the New Testament church emerged. On the day of Pentecost, about three thousand souls were baptized.

And they continued stedfastly in the apostles' doctrine and fellowship, and in breaking of bread, and in prayers. — **Acts 2:42 (KJV)**

There were principles that needed to be learned that were essential to the effectiveness of the work before the new converts. Acts 2:42 is biblical evidence that new converts were expected to learn what the apostles taught. The apostles attached themselves to new converts and impressed upon them the knowledge they were expected to adhere to while conveying the message of salvation. The word "continued" meant that the apostles did not abandon these new converts to speculate about doctrinal beliefs, but rather gave special attention to secure the value of the gospel of salvation.

John Phillips explains in his commentary *Exploring Acts* that there are certain markings of this infant church.

First it was marked by truth: "they continued steadfastly in the apostles' doctrine." The Holy Spirit was already beginning to fulfill Christ's promise that He would bring to the remembrance of the apostles all the teaching of Jesus and open their minds and hearts to new truth suited for the new age. First and foremost came the apostles' doctrine. It is no accident that this comes first. It always comes first. In all the epistles, precept comes before practice. Experience must always be tested by doctrine, not doctrine by experience.[19]

Preparing believers before they attempt to present the gospel is a biblical truth. Peter stated, "But sanctify the Lord God in your hearts: and be ready always to give an answer to every man that asketh you a reason of the hope that is in you with meekness and fear" (1 Peter 3:15 KJV). Peter emphasized the importance of spiritual principles that guide the life of the Christian. The heart of the believer should be connected to the heart of Christ. The believer should be ever prepared to defend the faith and give the answer for his hope in Jesus Christ.

The Apostle Paul makes reference to the believer's preparation on different occasions within the scriptures. However, he was most specific in his instructions to his young son in the ministry, Timothy. Paul instructed Timothy to prepare himself for the work of ministry to which God had called him: "Study to shew thyself approved unto God, a workman that needeth not to be ashamed, rightly dividing the word of truth" (2 Timothy 2:15 KJV).

Paul's instructions to Timothy were to prepare him for ministry so he would not distort truths. Truth is vital to the church and to maturing members toward evangelism. Untrue doctrine damages the development of new converts and causes them to repeat the untruths they have been taught.

Correction is a part of preparation. In Acts 18:24-28, Luke described a man named Apollos who came to Ephesus. He was a Jew who was a good preacher and eloquent in the scriptures. He was correct up to a point. He knew nothing about Jesus Christ. He only preached up to the baptism of John. Priscilla and Aquila took him aside and told him the rest of the story, and his ministry grew.

The biblical evidence shows that preparation is essential before practice is engaged. The focus of this material will be directed toward equipping and educating new members of the local church with basic biblical information that is pertinent to Christianity, before pursuing the work of evangelism.

Chapter 3 Questions

Question: How did Priscilla and Aquila correct Apollos to help prepare him? Who has come alongside you to help equip you in your ministry?

_____

_____

_____

_____

_____

_____

_____

_____

_____

_____

_____

Question: How did the apostles prepare new converts to share their faith? Have you followed a similar pattern in your own life? Why or why not?

_____

_____

_____

_____

_____

_____

_____

_____

_____

_____

Question: What role does the Holy Spirit play in Christians sharing the gospel? How have you seen this power at work in your own life?

_____

_____

_____

_____

_____

_____

_____

_____

_____

_____

Action: God has always required His people to know who He is and what His will for our lives is. Preparing believers before they attempt to present the gospel is a biblical truth. Scripture-based correction is a part of preparation. Untrue doctrine damages the development of new converts and causes them to repeat the untruths they have been taught.

Chapter 3 Notes

CHAPTER FOUR

Lesson One: Saved Solid

Am I Saved?

Nothing seems to be certain anymore. Within the last two years, I have had many personal friends and family members pass away. Not all of them were old. I said to a friend, "God is speaking, and if we can't hear Him, we are in bad shape." God is saying to the world that time is winding down. We are living in a day when nothing seems certain anymore.

Even the church is teeter-tottering on critical theological issues that define who we are as Christians. We cannot afford to be unsure. When we are unsure about what we believe, it places souls at stake. The old people in church that we laughed at as kids may not have had a sixth-grade education, but one thing they were sure about is that they knew they were born again. Now all of our educated folk aren't sure about anything!

In times like these, we need to be sure. With death's wheels rolling as they have been, you cannot be sure that God will not call you in the next twenty-four hours.

You may not know for sure how to solve the ecological problems and global warming. You may not be sure how to answer the hot-button issues that are debated on CNN. You may not be sure how to solve world wars that are rising on the four corners of the globe. But one thing you must be sure of is your own salvation, because time is winding down!

After the late John Wesley had been preaching for some time, someone said to him: "Are you sure, Mr. Wesley, of your salvation?"

"Well," he answered, "Jesus Christ died for the whole world."

"Yes, we all believe that; but are you sure that you are saved?"

Wesley replied that he was sure that provision had been made for his salvation.

"But are you sure, Wesley, that you are saved?"

It went like an arrow to his heart, and he had no rest or power until that question was settled.

Many men and women go on month after month and year after year without power because they do not know their standing in Christ; they are not sure of their own footing for eternity. Latimer wrote Ridley once that when he was settled and steadfast about his own salvation, he was as bold as a lion. But if that hope became eclipsed, he was fearful and was disqualified for service. Many are disqualified for service because they continually doubt their own salvation.

In every new members' class that I have taught over the last fourteen years, I began with the same question: What does it mean to be saved? There are often blank looks on the faces of the class attendants. Then someone will give an answer, "Uh, it means I am going to heaven."

The truth is, most Christians cannot answer this basic question. How can Christians witness about salvation through Jesus Christ if they cannot themselves explain what it means to be saved? It can be quite humbling when one declares, "I am saved!" and the response is, "Saved from what?" and silence fills the air. The issue of salvation is a hot-button topic, particularly when it comes down to the question, "Can I lose my salvation?"

Part 1 of this training didactic is designed to cover seven basic questions that the Christian should understand as they relate to salvation and its security.

- Why is there a need for salvation?
- How do I get the gift of salvation?
- Why were we saved?
- Can I lose my salvation?
- What does it mean to be Saved Solid?
- What are the dangers of salvation insecurities?
- What are signs of being Saved Solid?

Why Is There a Need for Salvation?

This is a basic question that many people cannot answer. To make salvation more comprehensible, one can look at it as "bad news" and "good news."

The Bad News

Perhaps one can grasp the concept of salvation when it is understood that we needed to be rescued. The following scriptures help us discover the urgent, critical spiritual conditions of our soul.

As it is written, There is none righteous, no, not one —
Romans 3:10 (KJV)

No one is right in the eyesight of God. Our hearts are not acceptable to God.

For all have sinned and come short of the glory of God —
Romans 3:23 (KJV)

We miss the mark in making God impressionable. We do not hold up to the standard God requires.

For the wages of sin is death — **Romans 6:23 (KJV)**

We will get paid for sin. What we justly deserve for sin is to be put to death.

If we say that we have no sin, we deceive ourselves, and the truth is not in us. — **1 John 1:8 (KJV)**

No one will escape. We are sinners by nature.

The Good News

We can learn from the proceeding scriptures that sin has ruined the hopes of our future. Left with the bad news alone, there would be a hell sentence awaiting us all with no chance of reprieve. However, the following scriptures reveal to us that God has not left us in a hopeless state of condemnation. These scriptures indicate good news.

> *But God commendeth his love toward us, in that, while we were yet sinners, Christ died for us.* — **Romans 5:8 (KJV)**

This passage means that God intervened on our behalf because of His love for us, and He allowed His Son, Jesus Christ, to die in our place.

> *For the wages of sin is death; but the gift of God is eternal life through Jesus Christ our Lord.* — **Romans 6:23 (KJV)**

This scripture has provided the sinner with an option. Although the first part of the scripture is bad news, it is joined by the conjunction *but*. Conjunctions mean that what's on one side of the statement will be altered by what continues after. This passage reveals that God offers us a gift of eternal life. One part of the passage offers death, and the latter offers life. At this point, the serious student would ask, "What is the gift, and how do I receive it?"

> *For God so loved the world, that he gave his only begotten Son, that whosoever believeth in him should not perish, but have everlasting life. — **John 3:16 (KJV)***

There it is! God gave His Son, and His Son is the gift that Romans 6:23 makes mention of. We often leave out the verse immediately following John 3:16, yet it answers the salvation question.

> *For God sent not his Son into the world to condemn the world; but that the world through him might be saved. — **John 3:17 (KJV)***

How Do I Get the Gift of Salvation?

Faith is essential to salvation. William Barclay says,

> *Faith begins with <u>receptivity</u> when a man is at least willing to listen to the message of the truth. It goes on to <u>mental assent</u>. (He agrees with the truth he has heard.) But mental assent need not issue in action. Many a man knows very well that something is true, but does not change his actions to meet that knowledge. The final stage is when this mental assent becomes <u>total surrender</u>. In full-fledged faith, a man hears the Christian message, agrees that it is true, and then casts himself upon it in a life of total yieldedness.[20]*

Consider the following verses as "good news":

He that believeth on him is not condemned: but he that believeth not is condemned already, because he hath not believed in the name of the only begotten Son of God. — **John 3:18 (KJV)**

That if thou shalt confess with thy mouth the Lord Jesus, and shalt believe in thine heart that God hath raised him from the dead, thou shalt be saved. — **Romans 10:9 (KJV)**

For with the heart man believeth unto righteousness; and with the mouth confession is made unto salvation. — **Romans 10:10 (KJV)**

And they said, Believe on the Lord Jesus Christ, and thou shalt be saved, and thy house. — **Acts 16:31 (KJV)**

For by grace are ye saved through faith; and that not of yourselves: it is the gift of God: Not of works, lest any man should boast. For we are his workmanship, created in Christ Jesus unto good works, which God hath before ordained that we should walk in them. **— Ephesians 2:8–10 (KJV)**

Why Were We Saved?

What is it the point of salvation? Why has God saved us? Did He save us to come to church and that's it? Many of us never think about why God has saved us, yet I contend that every Christian should understand the crux of the matter. The crux of the matter simply means getting to the point of it all. It also means expressing the heart of the matter. This section is tailored to teach the process of salvation, the powerlessness of self in the role of salvation, the present from the Savior, and finally the purpose of salvation. The critical question is: Why has God through grace saved you? What is His purpose?

Context

Paul wrote a letter to the believers in Ephesus to get to the crux of the matter. They were people like you and I who were already saved but needed Paul to clear up any misconceptions and clarify their understanding about their relationship with God and how God's gift of grace has blessed us. Paul described God's relationship with His people in the past, in the present, and in the future. Paul began with our past relationship, moved to our present, and finally concluded with our future relationship with God. Verse 8 of chapter 2 gets to the point of salvation, or the crux of the matter.

> *For by grace are ye saved through faith; and that not of yourselves: it is the gift of God: Not of works, lest any man should boast. For we are his workmanship, created in*

Christ Jesus unto good works, which God hath before ordained that we should walk in them. — ***Ephesians 2:8–10 (KJV)***

Let's examine four movements in the text.

The Process of Salvation

For by grace are ye saved through faith... — ***Ephesians 2:8 (KJV)***

There are three words we must understand here: grace, saved, and faith.

- **Grace:** the unmerited favor of God. Grace is God giving to us what we do not deserve.
- **Saved:** To be saved means that the Lord Jesus Christ has rescued us from God's wrath and judgment. Romans 6:23 clearly states, "For the wages of sin is death" (KJV). Yet Romans 5:8 teaches that "God commendeth his love toward us, in that, while we were yet sinners, Christ died for us" (KJV). Salvation by grace alone means that we did absolutely nothing to earn or merit salvation. Christ did it for us. We have been rescued from eternal damnation.
- **Faith:** Faith is the process. Salvation through faith alone means that we receive salvation through trusting in what Jesus did for us on the cross. Paul was not showing them how to

be saved but how they *were* saved. The process of salvation is having the faith to rely totally on what God has done.

The Powerlessness of Self

...and that not of yourselves... — ***Ephesians 2:8 (KJV)***

The point Paul is making here is that you had absolutely nothing to do with your own salvation. Look closely at his words: "For by grace are ye saved through faith; and that not of yourselves" (Ephesians 2:8 KJV). You may be thinking that faith is an independent act, but is it really? What Paul is emphasizing here is that the grace or power to believe and the act of believing are two different things. Grace allows you to believe for yourself and put that belief into action. Besides, if we could take credit for our faith, it would nullify Christ's independent work. God gives us faith to believe. Remember what Barclay said: First there must be receptivity, then agreement, and then surrender.

We had nothing to do with salvation because we were dead (Ephesians 2:1). Dead people are powerless to save themselves. Let me illustrate. There is a difference between patients in a hospital who are on floors two and above and the patients who are in the basement. The patients on floors two and up are receiving medication; they have IVs in their veins. Some of them may not be able to eat, but they are given food intravenously because they are alive.

But the patients who are in the basement are in the morgue. They don't need medicine or food; they can do nothing for themselves. This is the spiritual condition that we were all in. We were dead in our sins, and we could do nothing for ourselves. Salvation is all of God. We were dead and unable to respond.

The Present from the Savior

... it is the gift of God — ***Ephesians 2:8 (KJV)***

A gift is not a gift until one receives it. What God has given to us in terms of salvation is a gift. You cannot work or pay for it; it is simply based upon God's grace.

For God so loved the world, that he gave his only begotten Son — ***John 3:16 (KJV)***

Here is the crux of the matter, and I must ask the relevant or critical question: Why did God save you?

The Purpose of Salvation

For we are his workmanship, created in Christ Jesus unto good works, which God hath before ordained that we should walk in them. — ***Ephesians 2:10 (KJV)***

The word *workmanship* is a term for an end product. It is from the Greek word *poiēma* that we get the word *poem*, a piece of literary workmanship. It means the finished product, not in terms of the purpose of salvation, but in terms of the process to secure salvation. The process is finished, but the purpose is futuristic.

When Jesus rose from the dead, you were raised up to life with Him. When Jesus was established on His throne, the promises of God to you were seated, or established, with Him. If you believe in Him, you are completed in Him. That is the process, but in terms of the purpose of salvation, we are all still imperfect, uncut diamonds being finished by the divine Master Craftsman. He is not finished with us yet, but His work will not cease until He has made us into the perfect likeness of His Son.

We were created and saved for good works. We were not saved by works, but we were saved to do good works. Good works are evidence of salvation, not a precursor to salvation. When you see a church feeding the hungry, when you see a church caring for the poor, when you see Christians loving those who are unlovable, it is a result of salvation, not a means to salvation. You cannot improve on the process of salvation, but you can be a good product of salvation. God saved us to do good.

Application

One of the most spiritually dangerous beliefs is that you can save yourself and get to heaven by doing good. If that were the case, we would not have needed Jesus to do for us what He did on Calvary. I hear people say often that they are going to heaven because they do good. I have to debunk that myth today and tell you that the road to hell is paved with good intentions.

You can feed the hungry and clothe the naked, but if you have not received the gift of salvation and don't totally rely on God's grace, you will miss the mark. This passage teaches us that God was a solo act in our salvation, but He saved us for a purpose: to bring Him glory with the good we do while down here on planet earth. We do good not to be saved, but because we are saved.

The notion of doing good to be saved is what floods the minds of the world today. People leave God out of the equation and say, "I don't need God or the church because I treat people right." It's dangerous to dictate your own life when you did not create your own life. The text says that we are God's workmanship, created in Christ, which God has ordained before the beginning of time that we should walk therein.

Let me conclude with the story of a man who dies and goes to heaven. St. Peter meets him at the Pearly Gates. Peter says, "Here's how it works. You need one hundred points to make it into heaven. You tell me all the good things you've done, and I give you a certain number of points for each item, depending on how good it was. When you reach one hundred points, you get in."

"Okay," the man says, "I was married to the same woman for fifty years and never cheated on her, even in my heart."

"That's wonderful," says St. Peter. "That's worth three points!"

"Wow, just three points?" he says. "Well, I attended church all my life and supported its ministry with my tithes and talents."

"Terrific!" says Peter. "That's certainly worth a point."

"Only one point?" The man begins to sweat. "How about this: I started a soup kitchen in my city and worked in a shelter for homeless veterans."

"Fantastic, that's good for two more points," Peter says. "You are up to six points. You only need ninety-four other points."

Flabbergasted, the man cries out, "At this rate, the only way I get into heaven is by the grace of God!"

Peter says, "That's all the points you need. Come on in!"

Can I Lose My Salvation?

This is a hot-button issue across denominational lines. However, we must review what Scripture has already established.

*All that the Father giveth me shall come to me; and him that cometh to me I will in no wise cast out. — **John 6:37** (KJV)*

Jesus makes the claim on the security of the believer that He holds fast to those who have been saved. We are a gift that the Father gave to the Son. God has taken

ownership of us and entrusted us to the protection of His
Son.

And this is the Father's will which hath sent me, that of all
which he hath given me I should lose nothing, but should
*raise it up again at the last day. — **John 6:39 (KJV)***

The Message Bible by Eugene Peterson interprets this
text more clearly: "This, in a nutshell, is that will: that
everything handed over to me by the Father be
completed—not a single detail missed—and at the wrap-
up of time I have everything and everyone put together,
upright and whole" (John 6:39 MSG).

My sheep hear my voice, and I know them, and they follow
me: And I give unto them eternal life; and they shall never
perish, neither shall any man pluck them out of my hand.
My Father, which gave them me, is greater than all; and no
man is able to pluck them out of my Father's hand. —
John 10:27-29 (KJV)

The operative question for each confessing believer
is: Am I one of God's sheep, and am I truly a follower of
Christ? The hand of God is viewed in light of Scripture
as a place of protection: "My Father, which gave them
me, is greater than all; and no man is able to pluck them
out of my Father's hand" (John 10:29 KJV).

A shepherd who cannot protect His sheep is not
worthy of being called a "good shepherd," as Jesus says
He is (John 10:11 KJV). Jesus said, "I and my Father are
one" (John 10:30 KJV). God's love protects us. We are

His redeemed that have been saved by the blood of His Son, Jesus Christ.

"No man can pluck you" is assurance of the sovereign hand of God. Verse 30 is double security of salvation. We are safe and secure in the hands of the Father and Son.

The Bible describes each human being as one of two depictions: sheep or goat. In Matthew 25, there is a condemning scenario for the goats, yet a comforting situation for the sheep.

There are many people who profess to "once being saved." The question remains, were they really saved at first?

A. W. Tozer said, "When people find that after being in the church for years they are not making much progress, they ought to examine themselves and wonder whether they have been truly converted."[21]

*Verily, verily, I say unto you, He that heareth my word, and believeth on him that sent me, hath everlasting life, and shall not come into condemnation; but is passed from death unto life. — **John 5:24 (KJV)***

*For by one offering he hath perfected for ever them that are sanctified. — **Hebrews 10:14 (KJV)***

The Message version reads, "It was a perfect sacrifice by a perfect person to perfect some very imperfect people. By that single offering, he did everything that needed to be done for everyone who takes part in the purifying process" (Hebrews 10:14 MSG).

In whom ye also trusted, after that ye heard the word of truth, the gospel of your salvation: in whom also after that ye believed, ye were sealed with that holy Spirit of promise.
—*Ephesians 1:13 KJV*

It is from this passage that I am reminded of the sealing process that my late grandmother would use to preserve jelly. She would go through a manner of making sure that the mason jars were properly sealed so no outside elements would cause her product to spoil. In the same manner, God seals us through the Holy Spirit to preserve and protect our salvation.

What Does It Mean to Be Saved Solid?

We can use an acronym to identify through scriptures what it means to be saved **S.O.L.I.D.**

- **S**table: not likely to change or fail; firmly established.

A double minded man is unstable in all his ways. — *James 1:8 (KJV)*

- **O**rdered: given an authoritative direction or instruction to do something.

*The steps of a good man are ordered by the L*ORD*: and he delighteth in his way.* — ***Psalm 37:23 (KJV)***

*But the L*ORD *said unto me, Say not, I am a child: for thou shalt go to all that I shall send thee, and whatsoever I command thee thou shalt speak.* — ***Jeremiah 1:7 (KJV)***

- Loving: feeling or showing love or great care.

We know that we have passed from death unto life, because we love the brethren. He that loveth not his brother abideth in death. — ***1 John 3:14 (KJV)***

Beloved, let us love one another: for love is of God; and every one that loveth is born of God, and knoweth God. — ***1 John 4:7 (KJV)***

- Impassionate: strongly affected.

And they continued stedfastly in the apostles' doctrine and fellowship, and in breaking of bread, and in prayers. — ***Acts 2:42 (KJV)***

For I am not ashamed of the gospel of Christ: for it is the power of God unto salvation to every one that believeth; to the Jew first, and also to the Greek. — ***Romans 1:16 (KJV)***

- Dependable: trustworthy and reliable.

But none of these things move me, neither count I my life dear unto myself, so that I might finish my course with joy, and the ministry, which I have received of the Lord Jesus, to testify the gospel of the grace of God. — Acts 20:24 (KJV)

What Are the Dangers of Salvation Insecurity?

As introduced in a previous chapter, there are certain dangers of salvation insecurity that hinder our ability to make an impact on those around us and on future generations.

Diminished Witnessing Power

One cannot be an effective disciple for Christ if he or she is not sure of His promise of eternal life. Jesus promised that He would give power to witness Him and the gift of eternal life through Him. The promises of Jesus are what gave such a powerful impact to the early church at Jerusalem. Witnessing power within the early church soared once they received the promise of the Holy Ghost.

But ye shall receive power, after that the Holy Ghost is come upon you: and ye shall be witnesses unto me both in Jerusalem, and in all Judaea, and in Samaria, and unto the uttermost part of the earth. — Acts 1:8 (KJV)

Then they that gladly received his word were baptized: and the same day there were added unto them about three thousand souls. — Acts 2:41 (KJV)

Witnessing is diminished without faith, and no one will believe the testimony of one who is not certain of his or her own salvation. Insecurity will diminish your witnessing power.

But without faith it is impossible to please him: for he that cometh to God must believe that he is, and that he is a rewarder of them that diligently seek him. — Hebrews 11:6 (KJV)

Developing Insecure Disciples

Unequipped disciples are spreading like a wildfire, and it is incumbent upon pastors to teach the Bible and not rest on philosophies and the opinions of those who have not been properly trained. When a new convert carries the wrong message of eternal security, there is a danger of developing followers who have been misled and improperly trained to carry out the work of evangelism. This is how a David Koresh and Jim Jones could secure a following based off of their own insecurities and misinterpretations of Scripture. If you have a following of people and you are not secure in your own salvation, the followers will be just as insecure.

Damaged Doctrine

Circulating false doctrine has resulted in many fractions and splits among believers. When a person is not sure about his or her salvation, even though the Word of God gives clarity on the issue of salvation, the truth is distorted.

What Are the Signs of Being Saved Solid?

There are a few recognizable signs of being saved solid. The verse below reflects a heart of being serious about saving lost souls.

But when he saw the multitudes, he was moved with compassion on them, because they fainted, and were scattered abroad, as sheep having no shepherd. Then saith he unto his disciples, The harvest truly is plenteous, but the labourers are few; Pray ye therefore the Lord of the harvest, that he will send forth labourers into his harvest.
— Matthew 9:36-38 (KJV)

Another recognizable sign is knowing in your heart that you are saved and your salvation is stable. We see this in the following verse:

But sanctify the Lord God in your hearts: and be ready always to give an answer to every man that asketh you a reason of the hope that is in you with meekness and fear. —
1 Peter 3:15 (KJV)

Finally, a desire in one's heart to serve the body of Christ is a sure sign of being saved solid.

> *For as the body is one, and hath many members, and all the members of that one body, being many, are one body: so also is Christ. For by one Spirit are we all baptized into one body, whether we be Jews or Gentiles, whether we be bond or free; and have been all made to drink into one Spirit. For the body is not one member, but many. — 1 Corinthians 12:12-14 (KJV)*

When believers have a solid understanding of their faith and salvation, then they are ready to begin witnessing and sharing with others. This is when they can answer the question, "How do you know you are saved?" It is then that other souls can be won to Christ.

WORKBOOK

Chapter 4 Questions

Question: In your own words, what does it mean to be "saved solid"?

_____

_____

_____

_____

_____

_____

_____

_____

_____

_____

_____

Question: How would you explain grace, salvation, and faith to a nonbeliever?

_____

_____

_____

_____

_____

_____

_____

_____

_____

_____

_____

Question: Why is faith essential to salvation?

_____

_____

_____

_____

_____

_____

_____

_____

_____

_____

_____

Question: What does it mean that you are God's workmanship? How have you seen this play out in your own life?

_____

_____

_____

_____

_____

_____

_____

_____

_____

_____

_____

Question: Why is it spiritually dangerous to believe that you can save yourself by doing good? How have you slid into this mindset at times?

_____

_____

_____

_____

_____

_____

_____

_____

_____

_____

_____

Action: Many are disqualified for service because they continually doubt their own salvation. The process of salvation involves having the faith to rely totally on what God has done. We were dead in our sins, and we could do nothing for ourselves. God was a solo act in our salvation, and He seals us through the Holy Spirit to preserve and protect our salvation. You cannot improve on the process of salvation, but you can be a good product of salvation by bringing God's glory with the good you do. As believers, we need to have a solid understanding of our faith and salvation so we can be ready to witness and share with others, so that other souls may be won to Christ.

Chapter 4 Notes

_____

_____

_____

_____

_____

_____

_____

_____

_____

_____

_____

_____

_____

_____

_____

_____

_____

_____

_____

_____

_____

_____

_____

_____

_____

_____

CHAPTER FIVE

Lesson Two: Soul Maintenance Plan

Why Didn't They Come Back?

In 2008, I conducted a funeral for a young person at the church where I serve as pastor. I remember giving emphasis on the importance of accepting Christ before it was too late. While giving the eulogy, I told the story of a man who had been attending our church for several Sundays and would never join the church. He kept saying, "Next week I will do it." Unfortunately, the last Sunday he uttered those words would be his last day alive. His apartment caught on fire that Sunday night, and he perished in the flames.

After I gave the eulogy, I felt led by the Holy Spirit to give an altar call. In the tradition where I serve, we refer to it as "opening the doors of the church." That day, seventeen people came forth to join the church or to give their lives to church. The New Members Committee immediately recorded their names and gave them information concerning new members' training and other pertinent information to filter them into the life of the church. Needless to say, I was excited to have so many people join our church on that day. Through the death of the person being eulogized, God reaped a harvest.

I couldn't wait for Sunday morning to meet my new members in the New Members Training class. Sunday morning came and went. I never saw any of those people again. We tried calling, only to find out many had given false information.

The truth is, many people believe that if they join the church, that's all that's needed. They go through life saying, "I believe. I am converted. Isn't that enough? You mean I have to come to church every Sunday, too? I don't think so." They never weigh in the factor of actually being a part of the life of the church. Some really cannot see the need for the church and feel that it has no relevancy except for wedding, baptism, and funeral time.

It is essential that we do not leave the Christian at conversion. Conversion is the point of belief in the Plan of Salvation. However, it is imperative that Christians take responsibility for growth and development so they may become strong disciples for Christ. When one joins the church, there should be some spiritual maturation. The only way to accomplish spiritual growth is through a Soul Maintenance Plan.

This section is designed to emphasize the important role the church plays in developing one's relationship with God through prayer life, worship experience, and biblical knowledge. The goal is to increase the desire to attend Sunday worship, prayer meetings, and Bible studies as well as to become involved in ministry.

This portion of the training didactic is designed to cover four basic questions that pertain to spiritual development:

- What is the church?
- Why should I join a local church?
- Does church membership save you?
- What exactly does a Soul Maintenance Plan consist of?

What Is the Church?

As children, we often played a little "ditty" with our hands to describe the church. We would hold our hands together and make a steeple with our index fingers and interlock the remaining fingers and chant, "This is the church, and this is the steeple. Open the doors and look at the people." That was a cute little nursery rhyme, but it inadequately defines the church. The church is not the building. The church is made up of people that occupy a building. If the building did not exist, the church would still remain.

During the establishment of the early church, there were no steeples, stained glass windows, or cushioned pews. The church was wherever the people of God had gathered together.

As a teenager, I was given the definition that the church was the body of baptized believers of Jesus

Christ. It consisted of people who had confessed a belief in the death, burial, and resurrection of Jesus Christ, repented of their sins, and were publicly baptized.

> *Then Peter said unto them, Repent, and be baptized every one of you in the name of Jesus Christ for the remission of sins, and ye shall receive the gift of the Holy Ghost.* — *Acts 2:38 (KJV)*

The church is the *ecclesia*, meaning the called out.

Why Should I Join a Local Church?

That's Not the Way Church Folk Should Act

God has a very unusual way of developing the faith of Christians. It was 1996 and I was a new licentiate in the Gospel Ministry. I felt the power of God with me, I had just married my beautiful wife, and all was well with the world. Then it happened. A rumor was circling among the congregation that I was not the man I had portrayed myself to be. It was a rumor that could have been quite damaging to my new marriage. It was totally false, and it made me furious. It wasn't long before I found out through respected people within the church that the source of the rumor was an elderly lady who taught Sunday school, often quoted Scripture, and sang in the choir. I was hurt and shocked by her behavior.

With love, I respectfully approached her and made mention of what she had been saying and how it was hurtful to my wife and me. Right then and there I saw a side of her that I had never seen as she chided me about falsely accusing her. She walked away before I could say another word, ranting about how she had been victimized. She had, in times past, been so nice and sweet to me. What happened?

I later received a phone call from my pastor, who happened to be my aging grandfather. He asked that I would meet with him, and when I did, he informed me that the woman I had the conversation with had called him and accused me of "sassing" her and being "quite disrespectful." She demanded an apology immediately. I explained to my pastor/grandfather that I had been falsely accused and, as a matter of fact, she had slandered me.

The next few words out of my pastor/grandfather's mouth shall never leave my mind. He said, "I know you were falsely accused. I know you, and you have always been respectful. The problem is not with you and her. The problem is with her and me. She does not like me, so she figured the best way to get at me was through you. Give her an apology. She doesn't really care about the apology. That's not what she wants. She wants to get at me. God knows the truth."

I was quite frustrated, confused, and wounded. I was asked to apologize to someone who had offended me. I did as I was requested to do, and when I apologized to the woman, she turned up her nose and walked away without saying a word. To add insult to injury, whenever I would stand to preach, she would stand up in the middle of my sermon, cover her ears, and walk out. I thought to myself, "I can't believe church folk act like this." Why should I continue going to church if this is how Christians behaved?

That was twenty years ago, and the woman and my grandfather/pastor have long since passed away. As I look back over my ministry and many similar situations that have followed since the one with this elderly churchwoman, I now realize God's purpose in allowing me to be hurt by other Christians. God designed such pain in my life for me to develop patience, meekness, longsuffering, and other attributes that have developed my faith.

Christians must surround themselves with other Christians to grow. They will become a part of our spiritual maturation. We must be able to grasp the reality that the church is made up of people that come from the world. There are many different attitudes and personalities that clash in the church. Yet, it is by those occurrences that we learn forgiveness and to pray and trust what God is doing in our lives.

There is no such thing as an "Individual Christian Network." The church is the support of every Christian's spiritual growth. The church is where Christians come for maintenance of their souls, and to receive the necessary spiritual resources and attention so they may become a vital part of the movement.

Because the church is made up of imperfect people, the church is imperfect. I recall one minister saying, "If you ever find the perfect church, don't join it because you will mess it up because you are not perfect." The church is the vehicle in which the Christian finds expression of his or her faith. Why not join the movement that Christ died for?

The Church Stretches Your Faith

The experiences I have had in the church have not made me weaker; to the contrary, they have strengthened my faith. The church membership consists of people that have hurts that spill over into their personalities. When we are confronted by Christians who injure or trespass against us, we must have a forgiving spirit. This can often be difficult to digest, yet it stretches your faith. I am reminded of the hymn of the church by Horatio Palmer penned in 1868, "Yield Not to Temptation":

Yield not to temptation, for yielding is sin;

Each vict'ry will help you some other to win;

Fight manfully onward, dark passions subdue;

Look ever to Jesus, He'll carry you through.

Refrain:

Ask the Savior to help you,

Comfort, strengthen, and keep you;

He is willing to aid you,

He will carry you through.

Remember the challenging, "faith stretching" words of Jesus Christ.

Ye have heard that it hath been said, Thou shalt love thy neighbour, and hate thine enemy. But I say unto you, Love your enemies, bless them that curse you, do good to them that hate you, and pray for them which despitefully use you, and persecute you; That ye may be the children of your Father which is in heaven: for he maketh his sun to rise on the evil and on the good, and sendeth rain on the just and on the unjust. — **Matthew 5:43-45 (KJV)**

The stretching of one's faith forces change from carnal behavior and reactions to life's encounters to spiritual responses and behaviors.

Also, the Apostle Paul challenges Christians to stretch their faith:

Brethren, if a man be overtaken in a fault, ye which are spiritual, restore such an one in the spirit of meekness; considering thyself, lest thou also be tempted. Bear ye one another's burdens, and so fulfil the law of Christ. For if a man think himself to be something, when he is nothing, he deceiveth himself. — **Galatians 6:1–3 (KJV)**

Paul challenged the Galatians to do away with the old way of life and seek after the fruit of the Spirit. The nine characteristics mentioned are challenges for our faith to be stretched.

But the fruit of the Spirit is love, joy, peace, longsuffering, gentleness, goodness, faith, meekness, temperance: against such there is no law. And they that are Christ's have crucified the flesh with the affections and lusts. If we live in the Spirit, let us also walk in the Spirit. — ***Galatians 5:22-25 (KJV)***

The Church Strengthens Your Fellowships

In 2012, a member of our congregation was completely burned out of their home. That same year, another member lost his job, and his family was in dire need of spiritual support. Recently, a member of our church was tragically killed. In each instance—and many others that I don't have space to mention—the church came to their support.

It is unfortunate that many only come to the church for financial or spiritual support while they are in a crisis. Most churches do what they can with the resources they have. However, there is a common belief among many who are not connected with the church that the church is obligated to receive equal response to their distress as a church member. If we can reason for a minute, let's consider the people who sacrifice financially and spiritually as members of the church. If there are limited resources to begin with, should not the church members be given priority to those resources in the time of need?

The reality is that in the time of distress, church members respond differently to people they know and have forged a relationship with. That is not to say they do not respond at all to persons outside of the fellowship. It is the duty of the church to care for the hurting, the poor, and those in need. However, fellowships established within the church are more supportive when familiarity is concerned.

The Apostle Paul teaches that the church is the Body of Christ, designed by Christ to support its members.

For as the body is one, and hath many members, and all the members of that one body, being many, are one body: so also is Christ. For by one Spirit are we all baptized into one body, whether we be Jews or Gentiles, whether we be bond or free; and have been all made to drink into one Spirit. For the body is not one member, but many. — 1 Corinthians 12:12-14 (KJV)

The words of Jesus to His followers were given to strengthen the fellowship of believers: "A new commandment I give unto you, That ye love one another; as I have loved you, that ye also love one another. By this shall all men know that ye are my disciples, if ye have love one to another" (John 13:34-35 KJV).

We know that we have passed from death unto life, because we love the brethren. He that loveth not his brother abideth in death. — 1 John 3:14(KJV)

The Church Gives Stability to Life's Foundation

When I was growing up, there were many places I thought about going and many things I thought about doing, but I could not bring myself to go to certain places or do some things. One of the primary reasons was because there were many people within the church supporting my growth and maturity. Also, my pastor's teachings were often a source of conviction when I would behave in an un-Christ-like manner.

In 2004, a gregarious couple began attending our ministry. They were friendly and eager to get involved with ministry, but they never actually joined the church. I assumed they were married until they finally joined one Sunday. They had been living together for some time. Then came the challenging task of a pastor to address their cohabitation. Thankfully, from our sit-down they were able to see the biblical paradigm for man and woman living together. Within weeks they were married and became actively involved in ministry. More than that, they were given stability in their Christian pilgrimage.

Stability comes with pastor/member relationships, teaching and preaching biblical principles, and membership accountability.

The Apostle Paul mentions the protection of spiritual leadership.

Take heed therefore unto yourselves, and to all the flock, over the which the Holy Ghost hath made you overseers, to feed the church of God, which he hath purchased with his own blood. For I know this, that after my departing shall grievous wolves enter in among you, not sparing the flock.
— *Acts 20:28-29 (KJV)*

The Hebrew writer also emphasizes the dire importance of pastor/member relationships.

> *Obey them that have the rule over you, and submit*
> *yourselves: for they watch for your souls, as they that must*
> *give account, that they may do it with joy, and not with*
> *grief: for that is unprofitable for you.* — ***Hebrews 13:17***
> ***(KJV)***

The Church gives us stable citizenship in the House of God that is built on a strong foundation.

> *Now therefore ye are no more strangers and foreigners, but*
> *fellow citizens with the saints, and of the household of God;*
> *and are built upon the foundation of the apostles and*
> *prophets, Jesus Christ himself being the chief corner stone*
> — ***Ephesians 2:19-20 (KJV)***

The word of Jesus as it relates to His church is confidence of its foundational purpose in the life of the Christian: "And I say also unto thee, That thou art Peter, and upon this rock I will build my church; and the gates of hell shall not prevail against it" (Matthew 16:18 KJV).

Does Church Membership Save You?

We must be careful when people become members of a church where the goal is to move from membership to discipleship. The majority of people who become members of the church join out of emotion and have no intentions of moving beyond the status of being called a "member." They believe that just joining the church is enough. The Bible clearly states that judgment will begin at the church: "For the time is come that judgment must begin at the house of God: and if it first begin at us, what shall the end be of them that obey not the gospel of God?" (1 Peter 4:17 KJV).

We must adamantly teach that we are saved by grace through faith, and that grace should compel the believer to a victorious Christian life.

What Exactly Does a Soul Maintenance Plan Consist Of?

In order to grow spiritually, we must continue to strengthen our soul maintenance plan. This involves a commitment to dedication, devotion, and duty.

Dedication: Willing to Put God First

To dedicate means to set apart for some specific use. To have a soul maintenance plan means being dedicated to living life on God's terms. A soul maintenance plan says, "God, You can count on me!

*But let your communication be, Yea, yea; Nay, nay: for whatsoever is more than these cometh of evil. — **Matthew 5:37 (KJV)***

Devotion: Worshipping God

Devotion means ardent attachment or affection. To have a soul maintenance plan means that you are attached to the Creator of your soul and that you love God with your whole being. Soul maintenance consists of one's prayer life, worship, and study of the scriptures.

Jesus said unto him, Thou shalt love the Lord thy God with all thy heart, and with all thy soul, and with all thy mind.
— Matthew 22:37 (KJV)

Duty: Working for God

Duty is a course of action required by one's position. What you do reflects your position with God. How you live is a reflection of your love for God. God is love, and those who love Him have a love for His people. Concern for God's people is our duty. To have a soul maintenance plan means that what you do helps others. This is your responsibility as a Christian. Your duty to God and man is essential for the health and happiness of the soul.

He hath shewed thee, O man, what is good; and what doth the LORD require of thee, but to do justly, and to love mercy, and to walk humbly with thy God? — Micah 6:8 (KJV)

WORKBOOK

Chapter 5 Questions

Question: When was a time you were hurt by another Christian? How did it help you grow?

_____

_____

_____

_____

_____

_____

_____

_____

_____

_____

Question: How has the church given stability to your life?

_____

_____

_____

_____

_____

_____

_____

_____

_____

_____

_____

_____

Question: What are ways you can grow in putting God first?

_____

_____

_____

_____

_____

_____

_____

_____

_____

_____

Question: How can you improve in your prayer life, worship, and study of Scripture this week?

_____

_____

_____

_____

_____

_____

_____

_____

_____

_____

_____

_____

Question: On a scale of 1 to 5, rate how well you reflect your love for God in daily life. How can you take steps toward increasing in your love for God?

_____

_____

_____

_____

_____

_____

_____

_____

_____

_____

_____

Action: Christians must surround themselves with other Christians to grow. Stability comes with pastor/member relationships, teaching and preaching biblical principles, and membership accountability. In order to grow spiritually, you must be committed to putting God first, worshipping Him, and working for Him.

Chapter 5 Notes

_____

_____

_____

_____

_____

_____

_____

_____

_____

_____

_____

_____

_____

_____

_____

_____

_____

_____

_____

_____

_____

_____

_____

CHAPTER SIX

Lesson Three: Spiritual Gifts

What's Your Problem?

I had not seen Louise for months. I was an excited pastor when she joined our church and was eager for her to add her talents to our evolving ministry. She was an administrator in her professional life and had a grand reputation for pulling events, projects, and people together. She joined our ministry and seemed so excited to be a part of our church family, but all of a sudden, she went missing in action. I called her after she had been absent for a week or so. She assured me that she would be back to church soon.

After she had been missing for a couple of months, I called her to express that we missed her and that our prayers were that things were going well in her life. She honestly told me that she didn't know how she had become so detached from the church. Her words were, "One Sunday became two Sundays, and two became a month or so." She thanked me for calling her, as a few other members had, but confessed that she felt disconnected from the membership. I asked her how she would have felt more connected, and for the next five minutes she explained different techniques she would have applied to make members feel more connected to the ministry. It became obvious to me that she had a problem with the way our church provided membership services to new members that needed to be integrated into the life of the church.

That was thirteen years ago. Today Louise is the leader of the Membership Services ministry at our church. She discovered that her spiritual gift of administration lay within the area of the church experience that posed a problem for her. The truth is, your spiritual gift is usually discovered within some area of ministry where you see a need for change or help.

> *The two most important days in your life are the day you are born and the day you find out why.* — ***Mark Twain***

I once heard a statement that we were all created by God to solve a problem. When we discovered the problem we were created to solve, we would know our spiritual gift. Spiritual gifts are not decisions but discoveries. We do not pick our spiritual gifts, but God allows us to discover them. Mike Murdock states in *The Assignment*: "After all, the creator dictates to the created what it was created for."

I have discovered that most Christians behave strangely when it comes down to ministry and discovering their spiritual gifts for ministry. Why? Because spiritual gifts do not always evolve overnight. It takes effort. To make no effort to discover your spiritual gift is a sign of spiritual immaturity and selfishness.

Part 3 of this training didactic is intended to cover basic questions concerning spiritual gifts and provide five steps to discovering your spiritual gifts.

Spiritual Gift Basics: What Are They, and What Are They For?

A spiritual gift is evidence of grace given to individual followers of Christ by the Holy Spirit for the common good. A spiritual gift is given to Christians to assist in ministry. Ministry is meeting the needs of people for the common good. The first place in the New Testament that you encounter the term "spiritual gift" is Romans 1:11. The apostle Paul says, "I long to see you, that I may impart unto you some spiritual gift, to the end ye may be established" (Romans 1:11 KJV). The text is not saying that Paul wants to give them a spiritual gift; it is saying that he wants to share his gift. A spiritual gift is for the ministry of the common good.

The Greek word for spiritual gift is *charisma* or *charismata*. It comes from the root word *charis*, which means grace. This word *charis*, or gift, is used in the New Testament to remind the believer that it is only through grace that spiritual gifts are given. You cannot decide what you want your gift to be: God decides. You cannot force a spiritual gift on people. Proverbs 18:16 says that "a man's gift makes room for him" (ESV).

It is no surprise that the Apostle Paul made a big deal to the church of Corinth concerning the evidence of recognizing God's Spirit functioning in their lives. Ignorance is not an excuse for not discovering one's spiritual gift: "Now concerning spiritual gifts, brethren, I would not have you ignorant" (1 Corinthians 12:1 KJV).

God's various gifts are handed out everywhere; but they all originate in God's Spirit. God's various ministries are carried out everywhere; but they all originate in God's Spirit. God's various expressions of power are in action everywhere; but God himself is behind it all. Each person is given something to do that shows who God is: Everyone gets in on it, everyone benefits. All kinds of things are handed out by the Spirit, and to all kinds of people! The variety is wonderful ... — 1 Corinthians 12:4-8 (MSG)

God gives gifts to Christians for His glory and for edification of the saints. His glory is that which makes Him impressionable, and edification is that which makes one strong.

*As every man hath received the gift, even so minister the same one to another, as good stewards of the manifold grace of God. — **1 Peter 4:10 (KJV)***

*How is it then, brethren? when ye come together, every one of you hath a psalm, hath a doctrine, hath a tongue, hath a revelation, hath an interpretation. Let all things be done unto edifying. — **1 Corinthians 14:26 (KJV)***

Wherefore comfort yourselves together, and edify one another, even as also ye do. — *1 Thessalonians 5:11 (KJV)*

And he gave some, apostles; and some, prophets; and some, evangelists; and some, pastors and teachers; For the perfecting of the saints, for the work of the ministry, for the edifying of the body of Christ — *Ephesians 4:11-12 (KJV)*

Spiritual gifts are not for self-gratification, but to benefit the whole church.

But the manifestation of the Spirit is given to every man to profit withal. — *1 Corinthians 12:7 (KJV)*

God is the creator of all life, and God gives spiritual gifts for His purpose. There are many gifts, but there is only one giver and Spirit.

Now there are diversities of gifts, but the same Spirit. And there are differences of administrations, but the same Lord. And there are diversities of operations, but it is the same God which worketh all in all. — *1 Corinthians 12:4-6 (KJV)*

Does Everyone Have a Gift?

For every birthday that I can remember, I have received a gift of some sorts. Although there are people who unfortunately receive no gift to signify their day of birth, there is a differentiation as it pertains to spiritual birth.

> *There was a man of the Pharisees, named Nicodemus, a ruler of the Jews: The same came to Jesus by night, and said unto him, Rabbi, we know that thou art a teacher come from God: for no man can do these miracles that thou doest, except God be with him. Jesus answered and said unto him, Verily, verily, I say unto thee, Except a man be born again, he cannot see the kingdom of God.* — **John 3:1-3 (KJV)**

At the point of spiritual birth, known as conversion, God equips each believer with a spiritual gift to signify his or her new birth. It is a gift that all believers have received, a birthday gift from God, our Father.

According to 1 Corinthians 7:7, every Christian has gift: "For I would that all men were even as I myself. But every man hath his proper gift of God, one after this manner, and another after that" (KJV).

> *As every man hath received the gift, even so minister the same one to another, as good stewards of the manifold grace of God.* — **1 Peter 4:10 (KJV)**

According to Scripture, every believer has a gift even if he or she does not utilize it. No one gets a pass. If you are a Christian or confess to be a Christian, you have something that the rest of us need. The believer can no longer say, "I will just come to church and not get involved by serving in ministry." If you are not serving in a ministry, then you are not sharing your gift as God has intended. A gift exercised away from service always leads to confusion.

If every Christian has a gift, why are these gifts not being utilized?

> When I call to remembrance the unfeigned faith that is in thee, which dwelt first in thy grandmother Lois, and thy mother Eunice; and I am persuaded that in thee also. Wherefore I put thee in remembrance that thou stir up the gift of God, which is in thee by the putting on of my hands.
> — *2 Timothy 1:5-6 (KJV)*

The Apostle Paul admonished Timothy to "stir up the gift" (2 Timothy 1:6 KJV). The stirring up of gifts means that the gift Timothy had received was the Holy Spirit. That gift would allow him to preach, defend the truth, and bear fruit. The gift is represented by fire, and the notion is that if fuel was not added to it, it would soon go out. Paul was saying to Timothy, "Keep the fire burning. Fan the flame and don't neglect the gift God has given you."

Unfortunately, too much emphasis has been placed on naming your spiritual gift before you can use it. You should not worry about whether you can point to prophecy, lay hands on the sick, or discern spirits. The most important thing you can do to discover your gifts is to have a servant attitude. That is, ask yourself, "How can I best be of God's service within my local church?"

You will never discover your spiritual gifts by sitting on the sidelines or if you fail to follow through. You can't jump from assignment to assignment to discover your spiritual gifts. You have to jump in where you are needed so God can allow the process of developing your spiritual gifts. You may not have the same gifts as another, but God has unique gifts for you.

Five Steps to Help Discover My Spiritual Gifts in My Local Church

In order to develop your spiritual gifts, you must learn what they are. The first part of that process is to learn to take off your shoes and accept a posture of humility.

The Posture of Humility

In the book of Exodus is nestled the story of how God used one man as an instrument to bring deliverance to a nation. His name was Moses. God had a plan for Moses's life that would bring Him glory and bring His people into the Promised Land. We often look over the small details that lead to Moses's success. Yet, every detail is of vital significance. For instance, when we look at God's initial words to Moses, we fail to grasp its powerful lesson.

Moses was a shepherd tending his father-in-law's sheep on the backside of the Midian when he encountered God in a burning bush. Let's observe God's first instructions to Moses.

> *And Moses said, I will now turn aside, and see this great sight, why the bush is not burnt. And when the LORD saw that he turned aside to see, God called unto him out of the midst of the bush, and said, Moses, Moses. And he said, Here am I. And he said, Draw not nigh hither: put off thy shoes from off thy feet, for the place whereon thou standest is holy ground.* — **Exodus 3:3-5 (KJV)**

Don't miss God's instructions to Moses: "Take off your shoes." That is a menial request. However, if Moses could not submit to this small request, he would not have submitted to the weightier task that awaited him. What small assignment have you neglected at the church where you serve? Are you the member who sits stoically when the pastor asks the congregation to greet the visitors? Are you the member who walks past the paper on the floor, expecting someone else to pick it up? Or maybe you are the member who never comes to Bible study. To discover your spiritual gift, the first step needed is to take a posture of humility.

There are times when God will give us small assignments to test our humility. The critical question is: Can you humble yourself to do the small things? In order to discover your spiritual gifts, God wants you to take a posture of humility. The Bible speaks in narrative form about the issue of humility.

The fear of the LORD *is the instruction of wisdom; and before honour is humility.* — ***Proverbs 15:33 (KJV)***

Humble yourselves therefore under the mighty hand of God, that he may exalt you in due time — *1 **Peter** 5:6 (KJV)*

Whosoever therefore shall humble himself as this little child, the same is the greatest in the kingdom of heaven. — ***Matthew 18:4 (KJV)***

Humility is important, but there are other factors to consider as well.

The Principle of Availability

Over the last twenty years, I have observed a small core of members who are actually involved in the progress of the church. The majority of church attendees are overwhelmed with other life circumstances that do not allow them to become involved with the church ministry. As a consequence, ministry opportunities have been missed, unsaved lives are left in danger, and the faithful few experience burnout from the ministry.

The problem in ministry has not changed. There is a lack of availability. There have been countless experiences of asking someone to help with a ministry or church project, and the response too often is "I am not available."

Isaiah declared, "In the year that king Uzziah died I saw also the LORD sitting upon a throne, high and lifted up, and his train filled the temple" (Isaiah 6:1 KJV). When Isaiah saw the majesty of our Lord, his vision shifted from upward to inward, and he saw the miserable conditions of his own life. He said, "Woe is me! For I am undone; because I am a man of unclean lips, and I dwell in the midst of a people of unclean lips...for mine eyes have seen the King, the LORD of hosts" (Isaiah 6:5 KJV).

Also I heard the voice of the Lord, saying, Whom shall I send, and who will go for us? Then said I, Here am I; send me. — **Isaiah 6:8 (KJV)**

God needed someone who was available to spread His word. When Isaiah saw the majestic power of God and the miserable position of his life, he understood that he was nothing without God. He realized that if he would be worth what God had created, he had to do something. So when our Lord said, "Whom shall I send, and who will go for us?" (Isaiah 6:8 KJV), Isaiah said, "Here I am! Send me! I'll go!"

There should be something about God's majesty in the life of believers that motivates them to become available to do something for God. The problem with most people is that they try to squeeze God into their agendas instead of asking Him how they fit into His. We go through life viewing God as someone who needs to be available for our plans instead of us making ourselves available for His. How is it that we can call Him when we have a problem, but He can't call us when He has one? J. Hudson Taylor said, "I used to ask God if He would come and help me. Then I asked if I could come and help Him. Finally, I ended by asking God to do His own work through me."

Although one may come to church every Sunday, it is important to understand that attendance does not mean availability. Isaiah attended church, but until Uzziah died, he was not available. What or whom does God have to take from you for you to make your life available for Him? There are many people who have put out a "do not disturb" sign on their lives. They come to church and recognize that there is a need but would rather talk about the problem than be available for the solution.

There are people who have been in church so long that they seem sincere. They know all of the church protocol and paraphrases. If your life has not been made available to be used by God, what you do speaks so loudly that no one can hear what you say. Just because people do something often does not mean that they understand why they do it.

Ability without availability is a disability. There are those who have the ability, but are not willing to avail themselves, and it places the Body of Christ at a disadvantage. They have the resources and skill to help those in need, but for whatever reason, they will not make themselves available. The sad part is sometimes we only become available when life hurts badly enough.

What Does the Principle of Availability Look Like?

One Sunday after an afternoon ministry affair, I watched the first deputy superintendent of the Chicago Police Department, Al Wysinger, avail himself for service. He was the guest speaker at the church tea, and when the eating was over, he rolled up his sleeves and went into the kitchen to wash dishes and clean up. He didn't have to do that. I tried to stop him, and he said, "This is what I do!" He was not even a member of our church, but he made himself available. If churches had more members like that, we would be of better service to the community. We need to understand that servitude is not a step down, but a step up.

- **I Am Accessible for Service:** This means you have reached a point in your life where you realize that the key to life is serving and not being served.
- **I Am Ready to Sacrifice:** Ready for service means you have placed first what really matters. Remember, God has sent us here to solve a problem. We are on assignment, and to carry out your assignment, there will have to be some sacrifice. We all have a cross to bear, and Jesus said we must bear it daily (Luke 9:23). The Christian must realize that whatever sacrifice he or she makes in life, if it is not for the Lord, it will not register in the books of eternity.

- **I Am Willing to Be Sent:** Being available means, "I know somebody has to do it and if I don't do it, it won't be done!" How many people have been used to make an impact on the lives of others because they said, "Send me, I'll go"? When you say you will go, you are saying, "God, I know there is a problem to be solved, and I am available."

Make yourself available to help wherever you are needed, not because you are looking for something in return but because you genuinely want to help. Don't always wait for someone to beg you to help, and do not make people feel as though they can't make it without you. If you see a need to help with the children, make yourself available. If you feel a need to help with the operations of the church, make yourself available. If the door opens, walk in. If it does not open, find another door. One of those doors is where your gift awaits. Remember, Proverbs 18:16 says, "A man's gift makes room for him" (ESV).

And when the LORD saw that he turned aside to see, God called unto him out of the midst of the bush, and said, Moses, Moses. And he said, Here am I. — **Exodus 3:4 (KJV)**

And David said to Saul, Let no man's heart fail because of him; thy servant will go and fight with this Philistine. — **1 Samuel 17:32 (KJV)**

Also I heard the voice of the Lord, saying, Whom shall I send, and who will go for us? Then said I, Here am I; send me. — **Isaiah 6:8 (KJV)**

The Picture of Creativity

In 2004, the silver screen sensation *Ray* hit cinemas across the country. It focused on the career of the legendary Ray Charles. I found the film quite informative as to how the legend's career evolved. One scene that caught my attention was early in the film, when music producers were gently writing Ray Charles's career off as a loss. The problem was his lack of originality.

The scene that appears vividly in my mind was when Ray Charles was trying to launch his career and met opposition. Music producers told Ray Charles that the problem was he sounded like everyone else. He was good at impersonating Charles Brown and Nat King Cole. The producer's advice to Ray Charles was, "We already have a Charles Brown and a Nat King Cole. What does Ray Charles sound like?" It was when Ray found his own voice that his success soared.

God made us different. No one in the world has the same fingerprint. God took His time when He made us. The psalmist declared, "I will praise thee; for I am fearfully and wonderfully made: marvelous are thy works; and that my soul knoweth right well" (Psalm 139:14 KJV).

In my early ministry, there was a time when I wanted to be like everyone else who had great success. Yet, Psalm 139:14 made me ask the tough question: "When God has made me a first class presentation of who He designed me to be, why would I want to be a cheap imitation of someone else?"

Become a creative resource that brings innovative ideas to the table. Just because it has never been done does not mean that it can't be done. Ministry should be reachable, relevant, and real to affect this present age. God requires us to think of creative ways to get the work done. Nehemiah was creative. He created systems by dividing the work on the city walls into manageable sections with clearly defined tasks. Nehemiah's creativity was magnetic and exciting and inspired others to join in.

> *So built we the wall; and all the wall was joined together unto the half thereof: for the people had a mind to work.* — ***Nehemiah 4:6 (KJV)***

How do I discover who God created me to be and develop my own identity in Christ?

You Must Realize That God Has Made You a Creative Design

> *For we are his workmanship, created in Christ Jesus unto good works, which God hath before ordained that we should walk in them.* — ***Ephesians 2:10 (KJV)***

That simply means that we are His masterpiece and He created us for His pleasure, not for ours, and we have to walk in the purpose in which He created us. We are a special order that God has created "for such a time as this" (Esther 4:14 KJV). We must realize the originality of our design.

You Must Take the Responsibility to Cultivate Your Development

After you come face to face with who you are, you must develop the gifts that God has given you. Know yourself and to yourself be true. The beginning and the end of Psalm 139 give us a clue of how to do that. The beginning of this psalm says, "O Lord, thou hast searched me, and known me" (Psalm 139:1 KJV). Since He knows you, you must ask Him to show you the areas in your life that need to be straightened out so you can move forward.

The end of the psalm says, "Search me, O God, and know my heart: try me, and know my thoughts: And see if there be any wicked way in me, and lead me in the way everlasting" (Psalm 139:23–24 KJV). I remember that as a child I would hear older Christians pray, "Search me, Lord, and if You find anything that shouldn't be, take it out and strengthen me." To cultivate your development, you must ask God to show you who you really are, and He will reveal the weak areas in your life.

You Must Respond in a Manner That Says, The World is Waiting for My Contribution to a Dilemma

We often try many different avenues and imitate many people instead of discovering our authentic self. But the world is waiting for you. I am a preacher. I am not the best preacher, but that's who God made me to be. I am not a politician or a community activist; I preach! So all I think about is preaching. I didn't claim preaching; preaching claimed me. The problem arises when we try to do everything else but what God created us to be.

The Danish theologian Sören Kierkegaard says in his book *Purity of Heart* that the danger of simplicity is duplicity.[24] Put simply, we can't do one thing well for trying to do so many other things fair. James 1:8 tells us that a "double minded man is unstable in all his ways" (KJV). When you are double-minded, you can't find the stability to do what God has created you to do because you are being pulled by other affections. Don't make the world suffer because of your disobedience. Do what God sent you to do and you will sleep better at night.

Increasing Responsibility

In 2011, our church launched a five-year spiritual plan to seek God's direction for the future of our ministry. A small group of members became the steering committee to discuss how the church would respond to the will of God. Everyone initially appeared excited. However, as the years came closer to the final phase of the five-year project, only a small percentage of the steering committee seemed to take on the task of assuming more responsibilities. Most were comfortable with the small level of responsibilities with which they started. To discover one's spiritual gift, there must be a desire to increase responsibilities within the church.

Personal Responsibility

One of the responsibilities that should be enhanced in a believer is a personal responsibility to commit to spiritual growth. One's spiritual development does not only enhance the personal growth of the Christian, but it also contributes to the overall health of the church.

The personal responsibility to become consistently involved in Sunday worship, Sunday school, prayer meeting, and church functions is necessary to developing the spiritual gifts that God has equipped the believer with for the overall health of the church. When the Christian takes no personal responsibility to pray, study the scriptures, or devote time to the Christian life, they are suggesting that they are satisfied with what they know, what they are doing, and where they are in their spiritual development.

Personal responsibility requires each believer to move from membership to discipleship. When one becomes a member of the church, his or her goal should be moving toward becoming a disciple of Christ. Discipleship consists of personal development toward spiritual growth for the purpose of training others to become stronger in the faith. Why would God allow one to develop a spiritual gift when there has been minimal personal responsibility taken to discover it or to utilize it?

Membership Responsibility

Another responsibility that must increase is membership responsibility. As members of the church, Christians must take on the responsibility of participating in the overall mission and vision of the church. Paul reminds us in 1 Corinthians 12:4-7: "Now there are diversities of gifts, but the same Spirit. And there are differences of administrations, but the same Lord. And there are diversities of operations, but it is the same God which worketh all in all. But the manifestation of the Spirit is given to every man to profit withal" (KJV).

Every member has a responsibility to function in the capacity that he or she is gifted to assist the health of the overall body. I recall that the late Rev. Frederick Sampson gave this illustration: "The eyes cannot say to the feet, 'I'm pretty and I don't need you. You're ugly and must be covered up with socks and shoes.' The feet responded by saying. 'Well, try to get where you are trying to go without me.'"

The point is that every member has a responsibility to the whole Body of Christ if it is to function properly. Member responsibility warrants treating one another with Christian love, supporting church leaders, and working in unity.

Disunity is fueled by pervading ignorance of Scripture and inconsistencies among the saints. Nothing can stop the forward progress of the church like disunity. Disunity within the church makes believers unbelievable. Disunity is one of the most damaging things that can assault the church. The work is halted, the witness is harmed, and the worship is hindered. Dwight L. Moody stated, "I have never yet known the Spirit of God to work where the Lord's people were divided."

One way we discover our spiritual gifts is by taking responsibility to get along. There is power in unity. There's a reason God created geese to fly in a V formation. As each goose flaps its wings, it creates uplift for the goose immediately following it. By flying in a V formation, the whole flock adds at least 71 percent greater flying range than if each bird flew on its own.

Whenever a goose falls out of formation, it suddenly feels the drag and resistance of trying to go it alone and quickly gets back into formation to take advantage of the lifting power of the geese in front it. When the lead goose gets tired, he rotates back and another goose flies point. The geese honk from behind, not to complain, but to encourage those up front to keep up their good work.

Finally, when a goose gets sick or is wounded, two geese take responsibility to fall out of formation and follow him down to help and protect him. They stay with him until either he is able to fly or he is dead.

All we have to do to attract the un-churched to faith is for them to observe us acting like geese flying in formation. We must pick up congregational responsibility to travel in the same direction. We must pick up congregational responsibility to set aside our personal agendas and follow our leaders. We must pick up congregational responsibility to honk for our leaders, not honk against them. We must pick up congregational responsibility to not just coast in the back but take our turn near the front. When one of our members has fallen, either by sin or discouragement, we must not abandon them. If they'll receive us, we must be willing to stay with them, to strengthen them, to encourage them. As we do, we will soar to greater and greater heights and go further than we ever could have imagined.

Become a contributor. Contributors get the work done. A person seeking to discover his or her gift will jump in wherever needed without making excuses. The more we grow spiritually as good stewards, the more God will increase our responsibilities.

*Whatsoever thy hand findeth to do, do it with thy might; for there is no work, nor device, nor knowledge, nor wisdom, in the grave, whither thou goest. — **Ecclesiastes 9:10 (KJV)***

*The hand of the diligent shall bear rule: but the slothful man shall be under tribute. — **Proverbs 12:24 (KJV)***

*Seest thou a man diligent in his business? he shall stand before kings; he shall not stand before mean men. — **Proverbs 22:29 (KJV)***

His lord said unto him, Well done, thou good and faithful servant: thou hast been faithful over a few things, I will

make thee ruler over many things: enter thou into the joy of
thy lord. — Matthew 25:21 (KJV)

The Proof of Reliability

On Sunday mornings, I do not need an alarm clock to
wake up. I realize people are relying on me to come to
the pulpit with a word from God that was not thrown
together the night before. I understand that God is
relying on me to share in public what He has given me in
private. One should never anticipate God developing a
gift when an unreliable character is at hand. If one
commits to a task, others should not have to cross their
fingers in hopes of them following through. The efforts
of ministry are much more tedious and cumbersome
when persons of unreliable character are involved.

There was a much needed ministry within our church
that was initiated and implemented. The response of the
participants was promising. However, there remained the
question of who would lead the ministry. Growth within
congregations occurs when ministry leaders are
developed and become change agents to make a
difference.

As different persons were considered, one person
within the congregation agreed to take on the task of
giving strong leadership. Within a few weeks, signs of
unreliability began to surface. Meetings were scheduled
and canceled at the last minute, or the leader didn't
show. Promises were made of creative ideas that never

materialized. Nothing can thwart the efforts of ministry growth more than unreliability.

When discovering spiritual gifts, one must consider the following passage:

> *Again, you have heard that it hath been said by them of old time, Thou shalt not forswear thyself, but shall perform unto the Lord thine oaths...But let your communication be, Yea, yea; Nay, nay: for whatsoever is more than these cometh of evil. — **Matthew 5:33-37 (KJV)***

WORKBOOK

Chapter 6 Questions

Question: How does God use spiritual gifts to build up the church?

_____

_____

_____

_____

_____

_____

_____

_____

_____

_____

_____

Question: How can you take steps to discover your spiritual gifts this week?

_____

_____

_____

_____

_____

_____

_____

_____

_____

_____

_____

_____

Question: What are ways you can contribute to the unity of your church this month?

_____

_____

_____

_____

_____

_____

_____

_____

_____

_____

Question: Why is reliability important in ministry? How reliable are you? What are ways you can grow in this area?

_____

_____

_____

_____

_____

_____

_____

_____

_____

_____

_____

_____

Question: Spend some time reflecting on Psalm 139. Who has God created you to be for His glory?

_____

_____

_____

_____

_____

_____

_____

_____

_____

_____

_____

Action: A spiritual gift is given to Christians to assist in ministry. If you are not serving in a ministry, then you are not sharing your gift as God has intended. Be available to serve in your church.

Chapter 6 Notes

CHAPTER SEVEN

Lesson Four: Sowing Seeds of Salvation

The Gospels reflect the story of Jesus' earthly ministry, which spanned about three-and-a-half years. Within a three-and-a-half-year window, Jesus met twelve men and trained them personally to assist Him with His ministry on earth. Mark gives his account of Jesus's promise to the twelve that would follow Him wherever He went.

> *After John was arrested, Jesus went to Galilee preaching the Message of God: "Time's up! God's kingdom is here. Change your life and believe the Message." Passing along the beach of Lake Galilee, he saw Simon and his brother Andrew net-fishing. Fishing was their regular work. Jesus said to them, "Come with me. I'll make a new kind of fisherman out of you. I'll show you how to catch men and women instead of perch and bass." They didn't ask questions. They dropped their nets and followed. — **Mark 1:14-18 (MSG)***

He Caught Them

The King James version quotes verse 17 as follows: "And Jesus said unto them, Come ye after me, and I will make you to become fishers of men" (Mark 1:17 KJV). These were twelve ordinary men that Jesus used. They were not influential within the community but ordinary blue-collar workers. They were rough around the edges, cursing, hot-tempered fishermen. As much as we would like to paint the disciples as altar boys, it's just not true. They were a bit "gully" and knew their way around the streets.

It is interesting that Jesus spoke to these men in a way that arrested their curiosity and expanded their possibilities. Perhaps until this point, they thought it was normal to eliminate man from the fishing process, and abnormal to consider the possibilities of including man in the fishing perspective. Jesus caught the twelve hook, line, and sinker, and they became followers of Christ. He captured their hearts. This is a vital lesson, for the heart is the seat of one's awareness. When Jesus caught men, they dropped whatever they were doing and were "all in" for Jesus. Something was left behind to go forward, and there was a willingness to learn.

He Taught Them

Jesus did not say, "I will watch you be fishers of men or allow you to be fishers of men." He said, "I will make you." The making of the twelve was a three-year process that entailed strict teaching of the tenets of Christ followers.

Jesus was on a mission to teach the disciples how to further the gospel after He was gone. He knew His time was short, therefore His teaching had to be clear and impactful. The teaching began immediately. After Jesus came out of the wilderness, where He was tempted by the devil, He began gathering disciples and teaching them immediately about the truths of God.

And Jesus went about all Galilee, teaching in their synagogues, and preaching the gospel of the kingdom, and healing all manner of sickness and all manner of disease among the people. — Matthew 4:23 (KJV)

As Jesus saw His following beginning to grow, He climbed the mountain, and those who had committed to following Him sat down and listened to His teaching.

And seeing the multitudes, he went up into a mountain: and when he was set, his disciples came unto him: And he opened his mouth, and taught them, saying, Blessed are the poor in spirit: for theirs is the kingdom of heaven. — Matthew 5:1-3 (KJV)

In Matthew 5, Jesus began teaching His followers the blessings of followship, and how their new lives pertained to the kingdom of God.

All throughout the Gospels, Jesus taught His disciples about the truths of God. The teachings of Jesus were not mutually exclusive to the twelve. He taught in synagogues for all to learn of His wisdom.

> *And when he was come into his own country, he taught them in their synagogue, insomuch that they were astonished, and said, Whence hath this man this wisdom, and these mighty works?* — **Matthew 13:54 (KJV)**

However, there were times when Jesus taught His disciples alone. Jesus did not restrict His teaching to the synagogue. He used other methods of teaching to inject simple antidotes that His listeners could relate to.

> *And he began again to teach by the sea side: and there was gathered unto him a great multitude, so that he entered into a ship, and sat in the sea; and the whole multitude was by the sea on the land. And he taught them many things by parables, and said unto them in his doctrine...* — **Mark 4:1-2 (KJV)**

Jesus taught with stories that people could relate to. The parable of the sower was veiled in agricultural allegories that farmers could understand. After the teaching of parables, there were times that the disciples still did not understand, so Jesus took special "alone" time with them to open their understanding: "But without a parable spake he not unto them: and when they were alone, he expounded all things to his disciples." (Mark 4:34 KJV)

The twelve followed Jesus closely, and some of His teachings were without words. They would observe

Jesus early in the morning exercise prayer. All the disciples knew at this point was that Jesus would get up early in the morning and kneel in prayer, and that this practice of praying produced a power for which the disciples yearned. In Luke 11, the disciples began to ask Jesus to teach them: "And it came to pass, that, as he was praying in a certain place, when he ceased, one of his disciples said unto him, Lord, teach us to pray, as John also taught his disciples" (Luke 11:1 KJV).

Jesus taught the disciples basic tenets of being His followers, and it became a part of their personalities. He knew that His time was short. He would send them out alone to monitor their behaviors in His absence. He often tested them to see if they learned the lessons that He taught them. He would place them in certain settings where they had to exhibit the lessons that they learned. When He made His final departure, He sent them out into the world to continue what He started.

He Sent Them Out

Matthew 28:18-20 is the marching orders for the church to make disciples by teaching them how to make disciples. Jesus told us who He is, He told us what to do, and He told us how to do it. Every Christian should know this verse, for it is the mandate of the church. It introduces us to the Master, the Mandate, and the Movement.

After the resurrection, Jesus instructed the eleven disciples to meet Him in Galilee. As they headed in that direction, they saw Him and worshiped Him. Some held back because of uncertainty. Jesus immediately gave them a charge:

> God authorized and commanded me to commission you: Go out and train everyone you meet, far and near, in this way of life, marking them by baptism in the threefold name: Father, Son, and Holy Spirit. Then instruct them in the practice of all I have commanded you. I'll be with you as you do this, day after day after day, right up to the end of the age. — *Matthew 28:18-20 (MSG)*

Master

> And Jesus came and spake unto them, saying, All power is given unto me in heaven and in earth. — *Matthew 28:18 (KJV)*

A master is one who has power and one who is obeyed. Most of the time when people called Jesus "Master," they were referring to Him as a teacher or rabbi. We call Him Master because we bow in obedience to Him who has all power in His hands. When Christians experience hardships, there is but one who can alter the course of their calamity: our Master.

In Mark 4, the disciples were caught in a raging storm; in fear for their lives, they went to Jesus: "And he was in the hinder part of the ship, asleep on a pillow: and they awake him, and say unto him, Master, carest thou not that we perish?" (Mark 4:38 KJV). Jesus calmed the storm, and the response of the disciples was: "What manner of man is this, that even the wind and the sea obey him?" (Mark 4:41 KJV). Even the winds and the waves know that Jesus is Master because they obey.

A story is told by Jack London in his classic novel *White Fang* about a half-dog, half-wolf learning to live among men. White Fang loved chickens, and on one occasion he raided a chicken roost and killed fifty hens. His master, whom White Fang loved, scolded him and then took him into the chicken yard.

When White Fang saw his favorite food walking around right in front of him, he obeyed his natural impulse and lunged for a chicken. He was immediately checked by his master's voice. They stayed in the chicken yard for quite a while, and every time White Fang made a move toward a chicken, his master would stop him.

The master decided to test the dog's obedience by locking him in the chicken coop for the day. Locked in the yard and there deserted by his master, White Fang lay down and went to sleep. Once he got up and walked over to the trough for a drink of water. The chickens he calmly ignored. So far as he was concerned, they did not exist. He had learned to obey his master.

You know Jesus is Master in your life when you resist doing what you think you can get away with when no one else is around. In other words, your life has come into submission to the Master!

Mandate

A mandate is an official order by one in authority. Matthew 28:19-20 is a mandate, not a suggestion, for us to do something that the Master has commanded us to do. The mandate starts by telling us to *go and teach.* Jesus instructed His followers to go into the world and teach others about Him, to baptize in the name of the Trinity, and to teach others to observe their behavior so they may see what a Christian looks like. In other words, the mandate is to make disciples by teaching them.

Movement

A movement is a group of people who are working together to advance a purpose. Jesus's instructions were to start a movement. This movement consisted of passion, a plan, a purpose, and power.

- **People with a Passion:** Passion is strong and almost uncontrollable behavior. Passion is the energy that causes something to come to the forefront. When you find a group of people that are passionate about what they believe and about getting a message out, you have the makings of a movement. No movement can continue without passion. If you are a follower of Christ, you have to have some passion for what you do.
- **People with a Plan:** The plan is to teach people about Jesus and spread His message

wherever you may go. Jesus knew that people must be taught before they can begin teaching.

- **People with a Purpose:** The purpose of the movement is to save as many people as possible.
- **People with Power:** Any movement that lacks power can't survive. Jesus has promised us an eternal power supply to make the movement effective. He promised to be with us until the end.

Most people in church today will believe what they hear people say rather than what they learn themselves. The devil does not mind your coming to church jumping and shouting, as long as you don't learn anything. There is a problem when no one makes the effort to attend Bible class, but people feel a need to offer an explanation on how the church should be run. It is problematic when people quote Bible scriptures and don't know where to find them. Perhaps these are reasons why the church is not making disciples: We have moved further away from God's Word.

One of the biggest tactics of Satan is to keep people in the dark, because darkness prohibits a movement. Jesus knew the significance of bringing people into the light of truth. He said "to those Jews which believed on him, If ye continue in my word, then are ye my disciples indeed; And ye shall know the truth, and the truth shall make you free" (John 8:31-32 KJV). We have a responsibility.

Movements are critical. The last decade has yielded tremendous success for the LGBT (Lesbian, Gay,

Bisexual, Transgender) Movement that advocates for equality and acceptance for those who are a part of that ever-emerging society. The LGBT movement is active worldwide.

In 2009, the Tea Party movement began to flourish after President Obama's first inauguration, when his administration announced plans to give financial aid to bankrupt homeowners. Tea Partiers are known for their conservative positions and support of the Republican Party. The Tea Party movement gained momentum as they vehemently opposed every legislation that President Obama tried to implement, particularly universal healthcare. Various polls have found that slightly over 10 percent of Americans identify as members.[23]

In 2014, the Black Lives Matter (BLM) movement surfaced after the acquittal of George Zimmerman in the shooting death of a Black teen, Trayvon Martin. It emerged as a movement that campaigned against violence toward Black people, particularly brutality from the police. The movement received momentum after the deaths of Black Americans Michael Brown and Eric Garner by the police.

Movements are sustained by passion among those who find a common interest to be heard. The movement of the church seems to have come to a screeching halt. The church must ask the critical question: Are we a part of a movement, or are we in maintenance mode to keep the church relevant?

One question that many Christians cannot answer correctly is: Now that you are a member of the church, what does God expect of you? Well, the answer is not difficult at all. God expects for us to continue the movement that began with the early church.

The Church Movement

After the death of Stephen in Acts 7, the church movement accelerated with tremendous passion. We see the results in Acts 8.

We read about the death of Stephen in verses 1-4. His death sparked a great persecution against the church that scattered the saints. Luke makes the notation that Saul consented to the death of Stephen. Many new converts began to scatter throughout the region of Judaea and Samaria, except the Apostles.

Verse 3 tells us one of the main reasons why they scattered. Saul went on a "seize the saints" mission to create havoc for the church. He tried his best to destroy, devastate, and demolish the church. He would enter the homes of Christians, arrest them, and haul them off to prison. In Acts 26:10, the Apostle Paul said that some of them were put to death.

Although they were scattered, they continued to preach about Jesus everywhere they went (Acts 8:4). The strategy of Satan was to destroy the church through the scattering, but that was exactly what the church needed for it to spread.

Philip went to the Samaritans to spread the gospel (Acts 8:5). He was one of the deacons ordained in chapter 6. Jesus had been through that region before (John 4). The Samaritans were the link to getting to the Gentiles. Remember that Gentile means anyone not

Jewish. The Samaritans formed a link between the Jews and the Gentiles, for they were a mongrel people made up of both sorts, and held both Jewish and pagan rites.

In Matthew 10:5, Jesus told the twelve not to go to the Samaritans. When Philip preached, the Samaritans received him and great miracles were done (Acts 8:6). Those who were possessed were cleansed of foul spirits (Acts 8:7), "and there was great joy in that city" (Acts 8:8 KJV).

Ancient records give a very strange depiction of the man mentioned in verses 9-11. It is said that he pretended to be the father that gave the law to Moses, that he came in the reign of Tiberius in the person of the Son, that he descended on the apostles on the day of Pentecost in flames of fire, in quality of the Holy Spirit. What we are certain about is this man used sorcery, he bewitched the people, and he gave himself out to be somebody great. He confused their judgment by amazing them. He had them believe that he had great powers of God, and he had fooled these people for a long time. He had history with the Samaritans.But when they heard Philip preach, they believed him (Acts 8:12). Simon's tricks were no match for the Savior's treasure. God's Word is what made the difference. Philip preached the kingdom of God—that is, God's Sovereign Rule—and the name of Jesus Christ, and "they were baptized, both men and women" (Acts 8:12 KJV). Simon saw his fan base dwindling, so he believed as well and continued on with Philip (Acts 8:13).

When the apostles heard about the salvation of the Samaritans, they sent Peter and John to pray and lay their hands on them, "that they might receive the Holy Ghost" (Acts 8:14-15 KJV). As holy as the deacons were, they were still under apostolic authority. Peter and John came to Samaria, for the Samaritans had been baptized but had not yet received the Holy Spirit (Acts 8:16). "Then laid they their hands on them, and they received the Holy Ghost" (Acts 8:17 KJV).

Why Did the Samaritans Have to Wait for the Apostles Before the Holy Spirit Came Upon Them?

There are some who teach that you receive the Holy Spirit after salvation, but they ignore the transitional nature of Acts.

> *But ye are not in the flesh, but in the Spirit, if so be that the Spirit of God dwell in you. Now if any man have not the Spirit of Christ, he is none of his.* — **Romans 8:9 (KJV)**

There is no such thing as a Christian that does not yet have the Holy Spirit: "For by one Spirit are we all baptized into one body, whether we be Jews or Gentiles, whether we be bond or free; and have been all made to drink into one Spirit" (1 Corinthians 12:13 KJV).

Most scholars agree that God chose to do this as a special sign for a few reasons:

- **It Marked a Moment in History:** Because of the long history of conflict, this event was monumental.

- **It Was a Crucial Moment for the New Church:** The gospel has now spread beyond the Jews. It seems as though God gives them their own Samaritan Pentecost, as He appears to give Cornelius and his family an outpouring as well in Acts 10 as a sign of Gentile conversion. Normally, the Holy Spirit enters a person's life at conversion and baptizes, seals, and indwells that person, but this was a special event.

- **It Was to Confirm and Incorporate:** Peter and John came to these new believers to confirm them and incorporate them into the church. Philip was a deacon, and it would take the apostolic confirmation to confirm this transition in the formation of the church. This was a singled-out event and would not have to occur again. Peter and John gave credibility to the Samaritan spiritual movement. If the Samaritans had received the Spirit without the Apostles, they would have never come together with the Jewish believers. The rift would have remained, and there could have very well been two churches when God's design is for one church to flourish with one movement.

Evangelism Must Become a Movement

Part 4, "Sowing Seeds of Salvation," is designed to cover five basic questions concerning evangelism:

- What is evangelism?
- Why is evangelism necessary?
- How do we deal with the common fears of evangelism?
- What are the different ways to evangelize?
- What is the problem with evangelism?

What Is Evangelism?

The evangelism cliché is "one beggar telling another beggar where to find bread." Evangelism means to tell the good news about Jesus Christ and His plan for eternal life to those who do not know, so that they may come into a relationship with Him and become His disciples. Acts 1:8 instructs every believer that he or she has power to witness about Jesus Christ.

Chapter 1 of Acts records the last event of Jesus before He departed earth. The problem was that the disciples were concerned about the wrong things (see Acts 1:6). They wanted to know when Christ would make Israel an independent nation and free them from Rome. Jesus told them that the time was not for them to know. They were preoccupied with matters that were not important. However, Jesus told them what was important for them to know. He made a promise that they would receive power to witness Him all over the world.

But ye shall receive power, after that the Holy Ghost is come upon you: and ye shall be witnesses unto me both in

Jerusalem, and in all Judaea, and in Samaria, and unto the uttermost part of the earth. — Acts 1:8 (KJV)

Jesus's instruction to His followers was to be witnesses. However, people cannot bear witness to what they do not know. Evangelism is merely telling others the transformative impact Jesus has made in your life for the purpose of their own Christian conversion. Jesus expects us to be ambassadors of the Great Commission He has given in Matthew 28:19-20. The word "ambassador" means an official representative of the highest rank. We should be representatives of heaven.

The story is told of a man that lived high in the mountains in a wooden cabin. One cold winter night, as he warmed himself by his fireplace, he heard a scratch at the door. He went to investigate, and when he opened his door, he discovered a mangy dog who was so malnourished that his rib bones were almost protruding through his skin. He had open wounds all over his body that were evidence of being attacked by other animals. The man had compassion on the dog and took him in. Over the next several months, the man fed the dog and nursed his wounds. In time, the dog became a picture of health, shiny coat and all.

One day the man came home to realize that the dog was gone. He was heartbroken, yet went on with life. During the next winter, he once again was warming himself by his fireplace one night when he heard a familiar scratch on the door. He thought to himself, "I bet it's that ungrateful dog. I gave him a complete makeover, and when he was restored, he left me. I wouldn't be surprised if he is in worse shape than before."

He went to answer the door with a sense of indignation, and when he answered the door, he was met with chagrin. The dog appeared as healthy as ever, jumping up and down. However, the dog exhibited unusual behavior. He would run off the porch and to a tree, repeating the odd behavior. The man realized that the dog was trying to lure him to the tree for some reason.

The man came off his porch and approached the tree. When the man reached the tree, he was surprised by what he found. Behind the tree were seven more dogs in worse shape than the healthy dog was in when he first met his master. It became clear to the man that the healthy dog had said to the suffering dogs, "Come see the man that put my life back together. If he did it for me, he can do it for you."

We see a similar situation during the earthly ministry of Jesus in John 4. Jesus met a Samaritan woman at Jacob's well who needed a "life makeover." She could be considered "the much married one." She had been married several times, and life was not what it should have been for her. After her encounter with Jesus, her life was never the same. She became a one-woman missionary society. John records that she went into the city and told all of the men about Jesus Christ and how her life had been changed.

The woman then left her waterpot, and went her way into the city, and saith to the men, Come, see a man, which told *me all things that ever I did: is not this the Christ? — **John 4:28-29 (KJV)***

Evangelism is the ability to express the impact that Jesus Christ has made on your life.

Why Is Evangelism Necessary?

As a pastor, I have visited the bedsides of many who were dying. In some instances, the person was conscious and understood the witness I shared with them about Jesus Christ, and in some situations the person was comatose, awaiting death. The tragedy is that many people die without ever being introduced to Jesus Christ as their eternal Savior.

In 2012, a childhood friend whose wife was dying from a long bout with cancer called me to the hospital. Unfortunately, his belief was that if I prayed for her, she would make it to heaven. I prayed for her, but I also asked him if he was sure of his relationship with Jesus Christ. He was not. I explained to him that Jesus loves us and has already died for our sins. If we believe that He died for our sins, was raised from the dead, and now awaits us in heaven, we can be assured of our salvation.

I shared some personal experiences that I have had with Jesus and how my life had been forever changed. He assured me that he was on a mission to have a relationship with Jesus Christ so that his soul may be secured in heaven. Sadly, many people never think about their souls or eternity until they or their loved ones are at the point of death.

The fruit of the righteous is a tree of life; and he that winneth souls is wise. — **Proverbs 11:30 (KJV)**

Evangelism is essential for people to understand the necessity of being in a relationship with Jesus Christ and the plan and process of salvation. When the church has a movement of evangelism, Christians become "spiritual firefighters" delivering captives from hell's fire. In the Gospel of Luke, Jesus told a story:

"There once was a rich man, expensively dressed in the latest fashions, wasting his days in conspicuous consumption. A poor man named Lazarus, covered with sores, had been dumped on his doorstep. All he lived for was to get a meal from scraps off the rich man's table. His best friends were the dogs who came and licked his sores.

"Then he died, this poor man, and was taken up by the angels to the lap of Abraham. The rich man also died and was buried. In hell and in torment, he looked up and saw Abraham in the distance and Lazarus in his lap. He called out, 'Father Abraham, mercy! Have mercy! Send Lazarus to dip his finger in water to cool my tongue. I'm in agony in this fire.'

"But Abraham said, 'Child, remember that in your lifetime you got the good things and Lazarus the bad things. It's not like that here. Here he's consoled and you're tormented. Besides, in all these matters there is a huge chasm set between us so that no one can go from us to you even if he wanted to, nor can anyone cross over from you to us.'

"The rich man said, 'Then let me ask you, Father: Send him to the house of my father where I have five brothers, so he can tell them the score and warn them so they won't end up here in this place of torment.'

"Abraham answered, 'They have Moses and the Prophets to tell them the score. Let them listen to them.'

"'I know, Father Abraham,' he said, 'but they're not listening. If someone came back to them from the dead, they would change their ways.'

*"Abraham replied, 'If they won't listen to Moses and the Prophets, they're not going to be convinced by someone who rises from the dead.'" — **Luke 16:19-31 (MSG)***

The chilling verse in this passage is understood more vividly by the KJV version: "And in hell he lift up his eyes, being in torments, and seeth Abraham afar off, and Lazarus in his bosom" (Luke 16:23 KJV). The man in this story lifts up his eyes in hell and does in death what he should have done in life. He asked for mercy, and he has a great concern for others to be saved from hell's fire. He wants his brothers to be saved.

Perhaps if we all looked at the necessity of evangelism from the perspective of the man in hell in this text, we would take the mandate of evangelism sincerely. Evangelism is necessary to rescue those who are lost from eternal damnation to eternal life.

How Do We Deal With the Common Fears of Evangelism?

When the word "evangelism" is mentioned, Christians may become somewhat timid because they have already etched a mental picture of what they feel evangelism involves. There is also a fear of not knowing what to say. However, the Bible assures us that there is no need to fear doing the work of evangelism when we have been prepared and trained to carry out the task of evangelism.

The Great Commission charges us with "teaching them to observe all things" (Matthew 28:20 KJV). The Bible also instructs believers to be ready to give an answer pertaining to their faith: "But sanctify the Lord God in your hearts: and be ready always to give an answer to every man that asketh you a reason of the hope that is in you with meekness and fear" (1 Peter 3:15 KJV).

Christians should be always ready to defend their faith and declare their hope without fear of who they may share it with—but with a "fearful" respect of the one whom they confess their hope in, knowing that the operation of the Holy Spirit will empower them to witness.

But ye shall receive power, after that the Holy Ghost is come upon you: and ye shall be witnesses unto me both in Jerusalem, and in all Judaea, and in Samaria, and unto the uttermost part of the earth. — Acts 1:8 (KJV)

The Apostle Paul received the Holy Ghost and became bold in preaching the Gospel of Jesus Christ.

For I am not ashamed of the gospel of Christ: for it is the power of God unto salvation to every one that believeth; to the Jew first, and also to the Greek. — Romans 1:16 (KJV)

Chapter 24 of Luke's Gospel gives a dismal portrait of eleven terrified disciples. Jesus had already been crucified. Jesus appeared to the eleven disciples in His resurrected state. The disciples were terrified when they saw Him (Luke 24:37). He commanded them to go to Jerusalem and wait for the Holy Ghost (Luke 24:49). After the eleven disciples received the Holy Ghost in Acts 2, they became bold evangelists. There was something that happened between their terror and boldness. What was it? They received the Holy Ghost. The Holy Ghost gave them boldness to witness about Jesus Christ.

Observe Peter, who at one point did not want anyone to know of his association with Jesus because he was fearful that they would kill him. Conversely, after he was empowered by the Holy Ghost, he had no fear.

> *Then Peter, filled with the Holy Ghost, said unto them, Ye rulers of the people, and elders of Israel, If we this day be examined of the good deed done to the impotent man, by what means he is made whole; Be it known unto you all, and to all the people of Israel, that by the name of Jesus Christ of Nazareth, whom ye crucified, whom God raised from the dead, even by him doth this man stand here before you whole. This is the stone which was set at nought of you builders, which is become the head of the corner. Neither is there salvation in any other: for there is none other name under heaven given among men, whereby we must be saved. — Acts 4:8-12 (KJV)*

The key verse is Acts 4:13, "Now when they saw the boldness of Peter and John, and perceived that they were unlearned and ignorant men, they marvelled; and they took knowledge of them, that they had been with Jesus" (KJV).

The Holy Spirit gives us power to overcome our fears and to witness about Jesus Christ: "For God hath not given us the spirit of fear; but of power, and of love, and of a sound mind" (2 Timothy 1:7 KJV).

What Are the Different Ways to Evangelize?

When lives were transformed through Jesus, the person He came in personal contact with came to the reality of whom Jesus was. Subsequently, the individual became aware of how relevant His conversation was in comparison with the lifestyle he or she led while a superior alternative lifestyle with eternal rewards was within reach. Let's consider a biblical example of how Jesus shared Himself with others. There are many passages in the New Testament, but let us examine the setting and scene in John, chapter 4.

Jesus saw a need to go through Samaria, a place where there had been a long-standing rivalry between Samaritans and Jews. While in Samaria, Jesus was encountered by a Samaritan woman approaching Him at Jacob's well at noon, carrying her water pots. Assuming she came to the well to draw water, from the reader's perspective, this would not seem unusual.

However, from the viewpoint of a citizen in first-century Samaria, in the village of Sychar, this gesture of a woman coming to the well at noon would seem somewhat salacious. Most respectful women would either draw water early in the morning or late in the evening, when the women gathered at the well. The word "Sychar" is suggested by many scholars to be derived from the word "liar" or "drunkard" and could imply a city full of such men. In my own imagination, I would believe that noonday would be the most likely time that drunken men would be present, perhaps even by the well. The inference made in this passage is of a morally loose woman who came to the well against customary times to interact with the men of the city, perhaps the drunks.

Jesus broke a few customs of that day. First, he spoke to a woman, which was against Jewish culture. There was a rabbinical saying that a man should hold no conversation with a woman in the streets, not even his own wife, lest he become the source of men gossiping. Second, she was a Samaritan woman who came from a group of people that Jewish people detested. Finally, Jesus made a request of the woman to get Him a drink. This act would make Him ceremonially unclean by using her cup to drink from.

The woman was stunned that Jesus would approach her in an uncommon manner. However, the manner in which Jesus approached this woman demonstrates that Jesus removed any social barriers and prejudices of that day to establish a relationship with her. Jesus showed this woman His "realness." Jesus was not influenced by the customs of that day or the popular opinion of the community.

The woman came for water, and Jesus sparked a conversation with her about water, but not the water she perceived. Every word counted, and Jesus took time to make His conversation relevant to this woman's life. Jesus made the subject of water the lynchpin to capture this woman's imagination and attention, so He could continue a conversation and develop her desire for something better. It was then that Jesus made her aware that change was within reach.

She had never met Jesus before, but He revealed to her that He knew she had five husbands and was now living with a man who was not her husband. Jesus had her undivided attention. They talked about true worship. At the end of their conversation, she "left her waterpot, and went her way into the city," inviting the men to "Come, see a man, which told me all things that ever I did" (John 4:28-29 KJV).

The Jesus Approach

Jesus's approach could be described as real, relevant, and reachable. We are to model the ministry of Jesus. How can we emulate Jesus? Observe the Jesus approach.

Jesus was not like everyone else, but presented Himself as honest and authentic in His approach. He did not try to be someone He was not. Our most effective witness occurs when people can see who we really are. Although you may come from a different culture or community, "what comes from the heart reaches the heart." Be who you are and people will respect you.

In John 4, Jesus was able to detect an area within the woman's life where she needed some solutions to give her new life. Jesus showed that an alternative lifestyle was within reach that had eternal benefits. Jesus accepted people even if He did not accept their sin. The goal of evangelism is to show someone that a better life is within reach, no matter where the person has been or what he or she has done, and that coming to Jesus requires leaving something behind.

The Presence Approach

> *Ye are the salt of the earth: but if the salt have lost his savour, wherewith shall it be salted? it is thenceforth good for nothing, but to be cast out, and to be trodden under foot of men. Ye are the light of the world. A city that is set on an hill cannot be hid. Neither do men light a candle, and put it under a bushel, but on a candlestick; and it giveth light unto all that are in the house. Let your light so shine before men, that they may see your good works, and glorify your Father which is in heaven.* — **Matthew 5:13-16 (KJV)**

I was sitting in a restaurant on a Sunday evening with my wife, and a large group of well-dressed people occupied the table behind us. Their conversation was quite loud as they openly discussed the members in their congregation whom they were not fond of. There were alcoholic drinks in plain view, obscene language used, and a blatant disregard for church leadership.

Howbeit, there is nothing sinful about socializing or even taking a drink. Yet, Christians must be ever mindful of the presentation the world receives by their behavior. The presence of Christians in any given setting should have an effect that can be powerful without words being said.

Presence Evangelism is accomplished by honoring God with the way you live. One should influence nonbelievers to come to Christ by moral conduct. It is sometimes called Lifestyle Evangelism. It involves the charity you do and social action. Evangelism takes place long before we open our mouths to speak.

The Personal Approach

There are many people who take advantage of personal relationships they already foster, e.g., family, co-workers, neighbors. Making the good news clearly known in a one-on-one approach can be very effective. The personal approach of evangelism can be most effective when people we know are ready to receive the gospel.

For instance, when people receive a life-altering report, they become more receptive to hearing about God and His plan for their lives. This is not to say one should wait to witness until tragedy comes into a person's life. The Holy Spirit aids us in discerning the time to approach the subject of salvation in the lives of people close to us.

The Congregational Approach

Every congregation should make evangelism a priority, and there are many different approaches to do this.

In 2011, the Mount Hermon Baptist Church began a "Share Jesus Now" campaign. For an entire month, the focus of the sermon was on evangelism. Index cards were given to the members of the church on the first Sunday of the month. They were instructed to write to a person who they knew was either un-churched or unsaved. They placed the card on a visible board in the sanctuary called "The Most Wanted" board.

For three weeks straight, the church was in prayer for each name on the board. This was followed by a personal letter written by the pastor inviting the person whom the member placed on the board to attend church on the fourth Sunday. The letter detailed that our church had been praying for them at the request of their friend and they were invited to come to church on the fourth Sunday. The congregation strategically prepared for their arrival, and each portion of the worship was designed to introduce Jesus Christ to the guest.

Although there was not a tremendous result of people who joined the church, there were a few who became members. We are still working to improve this method. The point, however, is clear: The congregation should consistently be creative, strategic, and intentional in making their worship germane to reach the un-churched and unsaved.

What Is the Problem with Evangelism?

There is a shortage of people who are willing to do the work of evangelism. I call it a "shortage of personnel." Jesus said "unto his disciples, The harvest truly is plenteous, but the labourers are few; Pray ye therefore the Lord of the harvest, that he will send forth labourers into his harvest" (Matthew 9:37-38 KJV).

Here lies the problem. There is not an abundance of people who volunteer to do the work of evangelism. However, Jesus instructed His followers to pray that the Lord will send workers. Perhaps the problem with the lack of people to do evangelism is that the church has not made prayer of significant importance concerning the matter of evangelism.

Each member should have a desire to become serious about evangelism. There are three different views each Christian must embrace.

Personal Probing: Look Inward

The Apostle Paul was perhaps one of the greatest evangelists who ever lived. The biblical account of his conversion to Christianity reveals a man who was guided by his internal beliefs. Paul was a persecutor of horrific proportions to the Christians. He once espoused the legalism of Judaism and a cessation of the Christian faith. However, his conversion experience, documented in chapter 9 of Acts, reflects a fisher of men in the making.

Paul, who was named Saul, was at the peak of his mission to arrest and persecute Christians when he encountered Jesus Christ on the Damascus Road. Saul had warrants in his possession for the arrest of Christians when Jesus appeared to him and knocked him down, blinding him with a blazing flash of light. As he lay on the ground, blind, he heard the voice of Jesus asking, "Saul, Saul, why are you persecuting me?" (Acts 9:4 ESV). Jesus identified Himself as the one Paul persecuted. Paul was astonished and terrified.

And he trembling and astonished said, Lord, what wilt thou have me to do? And the Lord said unto him, Arise, and go into the city, and it shall be told thee what thou must do. — **Acts 9:6 (KJV)**

Jesus instructed Paul to enter the city, and then He would tell him what to do. Paul's companions could not hear Jesus nor see Him; this experience was personally designed for Paul to hear and see. Paul, having been blinded from the light, was led by the hand into Damascus by his companions. He remained there, blind, for three days. He ate nothing and drank nothing.

Jesus instructed Ananias to greet Saul, the former persecutor. With hesitancy, Ananias attended to Paul. Paul received the Holy Ghost and was introduced to the disciples. Paul began preaching the gospel of Jesus Christ. The rest is history.

One cannot help but think of the thoughts that went through Paul's mind during the three days that he was blind and without food or drink. Perhaps he began to review his past as a persecutor and how he had caused much harm to the Body of Christ. We do not know. However, it must be considered that Paul did some deep personal probing and took self-inventory of what his responsibilities toward Christ would be before he went forward with the assignment given to him: to preach the gospel.

Should this not be the initial step in every believer: to inquire what Jesus would have us do and take personal inventory? It is when we take personal inventory of our own lives that we realize our responsibilities to Jesus Christ. It's easy to criticize what others are not doing for Jesus. What have you, as an individual, done to prepare yourself for the ministry of evangelism?

O lord, thou hast searched me, and known me. Thou knowest my downsitting and mine uprising, thou understandest my thought afar off. Thou compassest my path and my lying down, and art acquainted with all my ways. For there is not a word in my tongue, but, lo, O LORD, thou knowest it altogether. Thou hast beset me behind and before, and laid thine hand upon me. Such knowledge is too wonderful for me; it is high, I cannot attain unto it. **— Psalm 139:1-6 (KJV)**

The psalmist concludes the psalm by asking God to investigate his life to examine what is needed to bring God glory. This psalm of inward probing seeks God so that life may become all that God has intended it to be for the psalmist.

Passion for People: Look Outward

Jesus had an outward understanding of the needs of other people, as demonstrated in Matthew 9:36. Jesus saw people whose lives needed ministry. No case was the same. There were different applications to address the needs of the individual. When He saw the crowds, He had compassion on them. The word "compassion" in the Greek is *splagchnizomai* [splangkh-nid'-zom-ahee]; this word means the stirring of one's bowels or the source of their emotions.

Ministry is not all about the individual, but about meeting the needs of others. In many cases, the same thing that deteriorates our biological family is deteriorating our spiritual family: We are merely coexisting under the same roof without any real sharing of life together. Compassion for others is the key to igniting evangelism within the church.

Evangelism takes on many forms. When hungry people are fed, naked are clothed, and spiritual needs of others become a priority, compassion becomes the key player that allows people to see the concern of Christians.

Petition of Productivity: Look Onward

Look toward heaven! There is a need for more workers to do the work of ministry. Why? That heaven may be full. The Christian is concerned about eternity. We focus too often on the here and now when we should focus more on the there and then.

In Matthew 9:38, Jesus gives a petition for more productivity: "Pray ye therefore the Lord of the harvest, that he will send forth laborers into his harvest" (KJV). Honesty would compel most individuals to admit to being deficient in the matter of personal evangelism. A shortage of personal evangelism within a church is crucial to its development. Evangelism is an act of desperation.

Individuals who have had the seed of the gospel planted in their hearts perform it. They have accepted Jesus Christ as their Savior, so they tell others about the Good News of Jesus Christ for the purpose of sowing the seed of salvation in their hearts.

Now that you are a believer, you have to be a worker. Workers bear fruit. As members of the Church of Jesus Christ, we have to be conscious that God needs more than believers. He needs workers who are willing to Sow Seeds of Salvation.

Chapter 7 Questions

Question: What are ways in which your life has come under the submission of Jesus? What are ways it hasn't?

_____
_____
_____
_____
_____
_____
_____
_____
_____
_____
_____

Question: How can you go into the world and teach about Jesus this week?

_____

_____

_____

_____

_____

_____

_____

_____

_____

_____

_____

Question: In your own words, describe what it means to be an ambassador for Christ. Why is it important to share the gospel?

_____

_____

_____

_____

_____

_____

_____

_____

_____

_____

Question: How has fear prevented you from effectively sharing your faith?

_____

_____

_____

_____

_____

_____

_____

_____

_____

_____

_____

Question: Think of a nonbeliever you regularly see. Using the real, relevant, and reachable model, how can you share the gospel with this person in the coming month?

_____

_____

_____

_____

_____

_____

_____

_____

_____

_____

Action: Jesus taught the disciples basic tenets of being His followers and often tested them to see if they learned the lessons He taught them. Jesus instructed His followers to go into the world and make disciples by teaching them. Evangelism is telling others about the transformative impact Jesus has made in your life for the purpose of Christian conversion. Sharing your faith should be done in a real, relevant, and reachable way.

Chapter 7 Notes

_____

_____

_____

_____

_____

_____

_____

_____

_____

_____

_____

_____

_____

_____

_____

_____

_____

_____

_____

_____

_____

_____

_____

_____

CHAPTER 8

Lesson Five: The Stewardship Lifestyle

As we come to the final chapter, it is essential to realize that each chapter lesson is sequential. "Saved Solid" is the first step to preparing a church to evangelize. The subsequent three chapters, "Soul Maintenance Plan," "Spiritual Gifts," and "Sowing Seeds of Salvation," cannot be properly effective out of the order given. Each chapter has been developed to facilitate step-by-step growth in the believer's life. The final step incorporates the previous four steps as a total way of life that responds with gratitude for the goodness of God.

How you see life is considered your worldview. Your worldview becomes the lens through which you see the world. It is shaped by your pre-theoretical commitment that Albert Wolters describes as the cultural soil, at the root of which is one's faith.

When I was teaching a course called "Christian Worldview" at Trinity Christian College in Palos, Illinois, a student asked me a simple question at the close of our first class. I had introduced different philosophers and time periods, and the student asked, "How does this all come together?"

The final piece, stewardship, helps to bring all of the other parts together. Stewardship comes last because it cannot be understood biblically from the worldview of an immature Christian. Many tense up when the word "stewardship" is mentioned, because the initial thought from the immature Christian is: "All they want is my money."

To complicate the matter, many churches present stewardship as a moneymaking campaign. In actuality, money is not the totality of stewardship, but only the challenging component to many who are developing in the faith. The aim of stewardship is to present to God a committed life. In fact, stewardship is not a campaign but a way of life. It is a lifestyle.

What Is Stewardship?

Stewardship is based on the awareness that all we have attained from God—whether spiritually, physically, mentally, or financially—is a gift from Him to us for a purpose. How people utilize these gifts is relative to their Christian worldview. A Christian worldview sees and interprets the world through the lens of Scripture. The maturing Christian evolves from self-centeredness to a life of gratitude when he or she understands the following:

- **Saved Solid:** Salvation is a gift from God that requires belief in the promises and protection of God and leads to appreciation of God's plan of salvation.
- **Soul Maintenance Plan:** Because of salvation, growth and development in faith and fellowship with other believers become a priority.
- **Spiritual Gifts:** The process of growth and development allows one to discover how God has gifted believers to help each other grow and expand the Kingdom of God.
- **Sowing Seeds of Salvation:** God's purpose and plan for salvation is to utilize believers to move with urgency to share the gospel of Jesus Christ for Kingdom increase.
- **Stewardship:** Lifestyle commitment to the teachings of Jesus Christ becomes the goal of appreciative believers because of their Christian worldview. Stewardship requires responsibility on the part of each believer to develop in the four preceding areas and embrace each step as a way of life. Stewardship is the total picture of a Christian living out of appreciation to God by utilizing every resource that God has provided.

To show God our appreciation for the many blessings He gives us, we must give back a portion of our time, talents, and treasures. Stewardship is not a program; rather, it is an attitude and a way of life that calls for believers to share themselves.

A steward is entrusted with the care and supervision of another's goods. There are biblical examples of stewards. In Matthew 25:14-30, Jesus gave a vivid description of stewardship. Jesus described an employer who was going on a long trip, delegating responsibilities to his employees while he was away. He gave one servant five thousand dollars, another two thousand dollars, and the last one a thousand dollars, according to their abilities to make him a profit.

When the employer departed, the first employee immediately went to work and doubled his boss's money. The second employee did the same. The third employee dug a hole and buried his boss's money. After an extended time away, the employer returned to see what profit his workers had made on his money. The one given five thousand dollars showed him how he had doubled his investment. His boss applauded him for his good work and made him a partner. The same happened to the second employee. Because of his due diligence and responsibility, he was also made a partner. However, the third employee who had buried his boss's money immediately started making excuses:

"The servant given one thousand said, 'Master, I know you have high standards and hate careless ways, that you demand the best and make no allowances for error. I was

afraid I might disappoint you, so I found a good hiding place and secured your money. Here it is, safe and sound down to the last cent.'

"The master was furious. 'That's a terrible way to live! It's criminal to live cautiously like that! If you knew I was after the best, why did you do less than the least? The least you could have done would have been to invest the sum with the bankers, where at least I would have gotten a little interest.

"'Take the thousand and give it to the one who risked the most. And get rid of this "play-it-safe" who won't go out on a limb. Throw him out into utter darkness.'" — ***Matthew 25:24-31 (MSG)***

From this parable come several elementary truths concerning stewardship. From a biblical perspective, it is essential to understand that the employer in this passage represents God. God has resources that He has created for His pleasure.

Awareness Principle

The employees in this passage were aware that the employer created the circumstances whereby they were each given a certain amount of money. Stewardship demands certain awareness on the part of the steward that God created everything: "All things were made by him; and without him was not anything made that was made" (John 1:3 KJV). The house you live in, the car you drive, the clothes you have, God created all material possessions you have.

The Acknowledgement Principle

Each employer acknowledged that the money he received was not his; it belonged to his employer. Stewardship requires acknowledgement that everything belongs to God: "The earth *is* the LORD's, and the fullness thereof; the world, and they that dwell therein" (Psalm 24:1 KJV).

The Appreciative Principle

Appreciation is best demonstrated by how we respond to what has been given to us. The third employee's lack of appreciation is clearly seen in how he handled his employer's finances. Stewardship says, "I appreciate the Lord allowing me the opportunity to utilize His resources."

> *In every thing give thanks: for this is the will of God in Christ Jesus concerning you. — 1 Thessalonians 5:18 (KJV)*

> *Every good gift and every perfect gift is from above, and cometh down from the Father of lights, with whom is no variableness, neither shadow of turning. — James 1:17 (KJV)*

The Accountability Principle

Stewardship says, "Lord, I am accountable. You can count on me to be faithful with what You have given me."

His lord said unto him, Well done, good and faithful servant; thou hast been faithful over a few things, I will make thee ruler over many things: enter thou into the joy of thy lord. — Matthew 25:23 (KJV)

Moreover it is required in stewards, that a man be found faithful. — 1 Corinthians 4:2 (KJV)

God gives each believer a responsibility to utilize His resources for the good purpose of the benefit of others: "Look not every man on his own things, but every man also on the things of others" (Philippians 2:4 KJV).

How Do We Practice Good Stewardship?

Stewardship covers every area of life. The traditional approach to explaining what stewardship consists of is still very much effective. Consider that stewardship is comprised of the sharing of one's time, talents, and treasures.

Sharing Your Time

On every Thanksgiving evening since the 1930s, many shoppers prepare to press their way to malls and appliance stores across the country for midnight sales, to participate in what retailers have dubbed "Black Friday." It marks the beginning of the Christmas season shopping frenzy. The modern term "Black Friday" has become a popular explanation that represents the point in the year when retailers begin to turn a profit and marginally move their finances from being in "the red" to "the black."

Eyewitness news reports overcrowded shopping malls until the early hours of the morning. Some make time to go shopping even if they are deprived of sleep or have slaved over a Thanksgiving meal all day long. Why? Shopping for deals on Black Friday is important to them, so they make time for it.

I would imagine that many churches experience a drop in Sunday attendance after Thanksgiving weekend because people are exhausted from the Thanksgiving activities. During a time when believers traditionally show their thankfulness to God, excuses are often made for why there is not enough time to worship, pray, or fellowship with the saints to strengthen the movement of the church.

How much of your time goes toward the advancement of God's business? What is your attendance like for prayer meeting and Bible study? Do you volunteer your time to the church mission? Are you available to help with church projects? Are you too busy for any of these things? Some will not readily volunteer for church activities because there is no pay. Some will not participate in evangelism, feeding the hungry, clothing the naked, or any church activity because they say they cannot find the time.

The Bible teaches us that making God a priority is important and that when we make time for God, He will make time for us.

> *But seek ye first the kingdom of God, and his righteousness; and all these things shall be added unto you. Take therefore no thought for the morrow: for the morrow shall take thought for the things of itself. Sufficient unto the day is the evil thereof.* — *Matthew 6:33-34 (KJV)*

Sharing Your Talents

A woman—let's call her Lisa—joined our church. On one occasion, she surprisingly appeared in the Easter program for a solo. Someone heard her singing along with the choir from her seat in the congregation, and asked her to play a role in Easter morning worship. Her voice was breathtaking, robust, clear, and melodic. That was the first and last time we ever heard Lisa sing. She was literally begged to join the praise team or the choir, but she refused. She said she didn't have time for that.

To add to the situation, she took on a bit of a celebrity attitude, as if her talent was beyond our small ministry. She said she might consider singing if some adjustments were made within the music ministry. Unfortunately, she was not receptive when I explained that her ability was a disability if there was no availability. She left the church.

In 2008, our outreach ministry formed an afterschool tutoring program to offset low reading scores within the community, as well as to provide a structured, safe environment for neighborhood children. There was a well-known lady within our church community who was a retired schoolteacher. She was known to be a successful schoolteacher and administrator and very effective in tutoring at-risk students. I contacted her and shared our goal to provide assistance to neighborhood children, and she agreed to help.

She attended the first day and ripped us to shreds. She was appalled at our lack of structure in launching the program. I explained to her that was the reason why we had solicited her help. Her response was, "Once you get it together, then you can call me and I will come back." Often people miss great opportunities to make an impact because of an unwillingness to share their abilities.

My mother is a spiritually gifted administrator. She has been blessed by God to bring together people and coordinate projects, workshops, etc. She retired from IBM as a very successful project manager. She uses her same God-given gifts to coordinate projects and workshops for the church. There are members who share both natural talents and spiritual gifts with the church without persuasion because they are aware that their abilities were given by God to promote His glory.

It is important to understand that talents are natural abilities, but a spiritual gift is a supernatural ability. Talents are encrypted in one's genetics from birth, whereas spiritual gifts are given at spiritual birth.

Spiritual gifts are a manifestation of the Holy Spirit in the life of a believer.

Both talents and spiritual gifts come from God. God gives talents to anyone. However, spiritual gifts are only given to Christians. Both consist of abilities. The personal question concerning every Christians is: Can the Kingdom benefit from my abilities, whether they are natural or spiritual? Are you naturally talented as a good administrator, singer, or project manager? How can your abilities strengthen others? Are you too busy to share your talents?

The problem is that many attend church but never share their abilities. Their willingness to help has remained obscure and fledgling. God has so designed the church where there is enough for everyone to contribute in some way. The Apostle Paul made this statement to the Christian church at Rome: "For I long to see you, that I may impart unto you some spiritual gift, to the end ye may be established." (Romans 1:11 KJV). The Apostle was not saying that he would give a spiritual gift but "impart" some spiritual gift. The word "impart" means to share. Paul wanted to share his gifts so that others may be strengthened.

Sharing Your Treasures

There is a sophisticated older gentleman within our congregation who regularly comes to church. He has been retired for several years from a very prosperous career and has financially prepared himself to be well off. He has money.

However, he does not attend any of the teaching classes that the church offers and is often disconnected from the preaching experience. His giving is bare minimum. He does not tithe, but faithfully gives in the offering. I once recall him saying when the tithe was explained, "Ten percent is too much money to give for the amount of money I have. It's too much." He loves the church, but he also loves his money.

God apparently wants us to know that there is a connection between giving and spiritual growth. The Bible offers about 500 verses on prayer and faith but nearly 2,000 on money-related topics. Why? Money is one of the hardest things for people to separate with, because they don't realize that it is God's money.

I recall a preacher giving this simple anecdote: "When you go to the doctor and he pokes and prods you, he knows that there is something wrong if you flinch when he pokes a spot that shouldn't hurt." His analogy meant that giving should not hurt, and when it does, there is something wrong. God wants us to view money as a blessing, and He does not want us to place it over Him. The Apostle Paul warns the believer about loving money.

> But godliness with contentment is great gain. For we brought nothing into this world, and it is certain we can carry nothing out. And having food and raiment let us be therewith content. But they that will be rich fall into temptation and a snare, and into many foolish and hurtful lusts, which drown men in destruction and perdition. For

the love of money is the root of all evil: which while some coveted after, they have erred from the faith, and pierced themselves through with many sorrows. — 1 Timothy 6:6-10 (KJV)

You cannot take money with you. The horror novelist Stephen King, who is not a Christian, made a compelling statement on giving. He said, "We come in naked and broke. We may be dressed when we go out, but we are just as broke. Stephen King, going out broke. Bill Gates? Going out broke. Oprah? Going out broke. Me, you, and everyone else are going out broke. Not a dime. All the money you earn, all the stocks you buy, all the mutual funds you trade—all of it is smoke and mirrors. It's still going to be a quarter past getting late whether you tell the time on a Timex or a Rolex."

Dollars have nothing to do with your destiny. Contentment is a learned disposition. The only way you can discover contentment is to realize that only Jesus can fill the void in our lives.

How much do you give? I did not ask how much money you tithe. The tithe is what you owe. The offering is what you give. Is it difficult for you to give money to the church? Is your cable bill higher than what you give to God's church? Do you find it extremely difficult to give to the church? If so, there is much room for your growth. Your financial contribution is needed to help the ministry of evangelism be effective. This is an area that requires faith and a clear understanding of the scriptures.

Every year, *Entrepreneur Magazine* partners with Price Waterhouse Coopers to put together a list of the

100 fastest-growing companies in America. The companies are no more than five years old but have annual sales in excess of one million dollars. According to the *Entrepreneur Magazine* "Hot 100" list, the number-one fastest-growing business in America was the self-storage business. In 2007, sales for self-storage were 109.1 million dollars, with some 52,000 self-storage facilities where people can store things that they don't even use. The fact that a storage facility made it onto the top franchiser's list is a sign that we have more than we need.

The Gospel of Luke seeks to draw the readers to the cross through God's abundant mercy and forgiveness. Luke challenges his reader to self-examination and sacrifice by taking a closer look at what it means to be a follower of Christ and an inheritor of the kingdom He proclaims.

In Luke 12:13-21, a parable comes as result of Jesus seeing an opportunity to teach some principles to His followers concerning their attitude toward material things. Jesus prefaces this passage with a caveat in verse: "Take heed, and beware of covetousness: for a man's life consisteth not in the abundance of things which he possesseth" (Luke 12:15 KJV). He tells a story of a rich farmer who has one of the first biblically recorded self-storage businesses.

The picture is very vivid. He wants for nothing because he has had a good career and stored up his bounty. He worked hard, and his hard work has paid off. He started with a small bumper crop, but it expanded. As his career "blew up" and he outgrew one barn, he would build another to store all of his assets.

By his own standards as a shrewd businessman, he had worked his way to the top. His concerns were selfish. His career was successful, but his conclusion was surprising. He goes through life storing, storing, storing, and never once entertains the thought of helping others. His basic flaw is in focusing completely on his wealth and on his own enjoyment.

Unfortunately, once he gets to a place of abundance and decides to retire, he suddenly and surprisingly dies. All that he worked for could not benefit him in the life to come! God calls him a "fool" because he has stored up all of his investments in a barn and has made no preparation for the life to come. God demanded his soul on the night that he reached the point where he thought he could enjoy his life's accomplishments.

There is a mindset that ever permeates the United States: "I got mine; now you get yours the best way you know how!" The truth of the matter is that success in the sight of God is determined by how you share that success with someone else. Jesus taught in the Sermon on the Mount that your fruits reveal who you are.

*Ye shall know them by their fruits. Do men gather grapes of thorns, or figs of thistles? Even so every good tree bringeth forth good fruit; but a corrupt tree bringeth forth evil fruit. A good tree cannot bring forth evil fruit; neither can a corrupt tree bring forth good fruit. — **Matthew 7:16-18 (KJV)***

It is not enough merely to hear His words; the words must also be put into practice.

The parable of the farmer teaches a clear lesson that at the end what really matters is your giving relationship toward God. One of the reasons Jesus gives for investing in heavenly treasure is that such investment is completely safe from loss. He points out in Matthew 6:19-20 that earthly treasure is always subject to uncertainty. Rust, moths, and thieves can destroy everything you have. But when you are rich toward God, you are investing in a heavenly account.

For what shall it profit a man, if he shall gain the whole world, and lose his own soul? — **Mark 8:36 (KJV)**

The Crux of the Matter

- God expects your *Adoration* toward Him, the Giver.
- God expects *Accountability* of the goods He has given.
- God expects you to have a healthy *Attitude* toward giving to the work of the Church.

Adoration Toward God

God wants you to have holy adoration toward Him, the Giver. We must realize that everything belongs to God.

*All things were made by him; and without him was not any
thing made that was made. — **John 1:3 (KJV)***

*The earth is the LORD'S, and the fullness thereof; the world,
and they that dwell therein. — **Psalm 24:1 (KJV)***

*And Abel, he also brought of the firstlings of his flock and
of the fat thereof. And the LORD had respect unto Abel and
to his offering: But unto Cain and to his offering he had not
respect. And Cain was very wroth, and his countenance
fell. — **Genesis 4:4-5 (KJV)***

God expects your love toward Him to result in your
giving being an act of adoration, not just
acknowledgment.

Heavenly Accountability

God will hold us accountable for the resources He has
given. He gives us resources to help others through
ministry. We are held accountable to do ministry.

*Then shall he answer them, saying, Verily I say unto you,
Inasmuch as ye did it not to one of the least of these, ye did
it not to me. — **Matthew 25:45 (KJV)***

Healthy Attitude About Giving

God does not expect us to be angry when sharing our resources. He requires of us to give cheerfully, systematically, liberally, sacrificially, and repeatedly.

- **Cheerfully:** "Every man according as he purposeth in his heart, so let him give; not grudgingly, or of necessity: for God loveth a cheerful giver" (2 Corinthians 9:7 KJV).
- **Systematically:** "Now concerning the collection for the saints, as I have given order to the churches of Galatia, even so do ye. Upon the first day of the week let every one of you lay by him in store, as God hath prospered him, that there be no gatherings when I come" (1 Corinthians 16:1-2 KJV).
- **Liberally:** "Moreover, brethren, we do you to wit of the grace of God bestowed on the churches of Macedonia; How that in a great trial of affliction the abundance of their joy and their deep poverty abounded unto the riches of their liberality" (2 Corinthians 8:1-2 KJV).
- **Sacrificially:** "And this they did, not as we hoped, but first gave their own selves to the Lord, and unto us by the will of God" (2 Corinthians 8:5 KJV).
- **Repeatedly:** "Give, and it shall be given unto you; good measure, pressed down, and shaken

together, and running over, shall men give into your bosom. For with the same measure that ye mete withal it shall be measured to you again" (Luke 6:38 KJV).

It is important for us to remember that this is God's world and these are God's resources. It is immature to think in terms of, "These are my resources." Whatever you have, it has been given to you from God to help someone else.

Finally, if you can change the way you think about your time, talents, and treasure, you can change your life. Become a river, not a reservoir. A reservoir collects water while a river, by the design of God, delivers it. Water flows through a river but stagnates in a reservoir.

Reservoirs have no place in the agronomy of the Kingdom. God expects us to be rivers so He can deliver His resources through us to others. This process makes us rich toward God. When one becomes rich toward God, he or she invests in the Kingdom of God.

A witty story is told of a man who would never give. He had talents he would not share, time he would not give, and treasures that he would not release. He went to church, but he was so tight that he could make a penny holler. He was a contractor, but the church he attended was falling down. He was an expert, yet he never assisted the young people who were striving to get into his field. He was loaded financially, but the church he attended was falling down all around.

He picked out the scriptures that he wanted to hear. He tuned out Malachi 3:10. He tuned out Matthew 25.

He tuned out Matthew 6. But he always talked about John 14 when Jesus said, "I go away to prepare a mansion for you!" All he talked about on his deathbed was his mansion.

When he reached the Pearly Gates, Saint Peter met him. He was excited to get to his mansion. Saint Peter began to walk him down the streets of gold. There were mansions on the right and left. He started singing, "I've got a mansion over in Zion, and it's mine!"

As Peter got down the first street, the man started asking, "Is that my mansion over there?" Saint Peter didn't say a word. They got a little further along, and six or seven times the man asked Peter, "Is that my mansion over there?" Saint Peter never said a word.

They were coming to the end of the streets paved with gold, and the man became worried because he saw the quality of the mansions going down. Finally Saint Peter said, "The one over there in the corner is yours."

The man said, "You mean to tell me that the little incomplete, small mansion is mine? I demand an explanation!"

Saint Peter said, "If you had sent more up here to work with while you were living, you would have had more to live in when you died!"

WORKBOOK

Chapter 8 Questions

Question: On a scale of 1 to 5, rate how well you are aware of, acknowledge, appreciate, and are accountable for all God has given you. In which areas do you need to grow? How can you do this in the coming week?

_____

_____

_____

_____

_____

_____

_____

_____

_____

_____

_____

Question: Stewardship is comprised of the sharing of one's time, talents, and money. In which area do you need the most growth? What are steps you can take to do this?

_____

_____

_____

_____

_____

_____

_____

_____

_____

_____

_____

Question: How can you use what God has given you to help someone else today?

_____

_____

_____

_____

_____

_____

_____

_____

_____

_____

_____

Question: What does it look like to give cheerfully, systematically, liberally, sacrificially, and repeatedly?

_____

_____

_____

_____

_____

_____

_____

_____

_____

_____

_____

Question: What do you often use to fill the void in your life? What are things that lead you toward discontentment? How can you take steps toward contentment in Christ today?

_____

_____

_____

_____

_____

_____

_____

_____

_____

Action: Stewardship is not a program; rather, it is an attitude and way of life that calls for believers to share themselves. The only way you can discover contentment is to realize that only Jesus can fill the void in our lives. God gives us resources to help others through ministry, and He will hold us accountable for the resources He gives us.

Chapter 8 Notes

_____

_____

_____

_____

_____

_____

_____

_____

_____

_____

_____

_____

_____

_____

_____

_____

_____

_____

_____

_____

CONCLUSION

Prepared to Defend the Faith

To counter a culture of untrained disciples, the church must return to basic biblical teaching, and this must become a priority within the local church. Scripture has proven that God requires His people to know about Him. Throughout the Old Testament and the New Testament, the believer is charged to learn about God.

My people are destroyed for lack of knowledge: because thou hast rejected knowledge, I will also reject thee, that thou shalt be no priest to me: seeing thou hast forgotten the law of thy God, I will also forget thy children. — **Hosea 4:6 (KJV)**

Therefore my people are gone into captivity, because they have no knowledge: and their honourable men are famished, and their multitude dried up with thirst. — **Isaiah 5:13 (KJV)**

Knowledge of God has never been relaxed for those who follow Him. God has always required His people to know who He is and what His will and word for our lives are. God has promised blessings for those who know of Him: "Blessed is the man that walketh not in the counsel of the ungodly, nor standeth in the way of sinners, nor sitteth in the seat of the scornful. But his delight is in the law of the LORD; and in his law doth he meditate day and night" (Psalm 1:1-2 KJV).

This theme continues into the New Testament. Jesus said, "Take my yoke upon you, and learn of me; for I am meek and lowly in heart: and ye shall find rest unto your souls" (Matthew 11:29 KJV).

Evangelism, biblically ascribed in the context of the New Testament church, pertained to followers of Jesus Christ who embraced a lifestyle that led to opportunities to share the gospel, or "good news," of salvation through Jesus Christ. However, it is evident in the Acts of the Holy Spirit that new converts were trained before they were deployed to serve.

Thousands of converts were baptized as the New Testament church emerged. On the day of Pentecost, about three thousand souls were baptized, and "they continued stedfastly in the apostles' doctrine and fellowship, and in breaking of bread, and in prayers" (Acts 2:41-42 KJV). There were principles to be learned that were essential to the effectiveness of the work before the new converts.

Acts 2:42 is biblical evidence that new converts were expected to learn what the apostles taught. The apostles attached themselves to new converts, impressing upon them the knowledge that they were expected to adhere to while conveying the message of salvation. The word "continued" meant that the apostles did not abandon these new converts to speculate about doctrinal beliefs, but rather gave them special attention to secure the value of the gospel of salvation.

The Apostle Paul made reference to the believer's preparation on different occasions within the scriptures. However, he was most specific in his instructions to his young son in the ministry, Timothy. Paul instructed Timothy to prepare himself for the work of ministry to which God had called him: "Study to shew thyself approved unto God, a workman that needeth not to be ashamed, rightly dividing the word of truth" (2 Timothy 2:15 KJV).

Paul's instructions to Timothy were to prepare him for ministry so he would not distort truths. Truth is vital to the church and to maturing members toward evangelism. Untrue doctrine damages the development of new converts and causes them to repeat the untruths they have been taught.

Preparing believers before they attempt to present the gospel is a biblical truth.

But sanctify the Lord God in your hearts: and be ready always to give an answer to every man that asketh you a reason of the hope that is in you with meekness and fear —
1 Peter 3:15 (KJV)

The heart of the believer should be connected to the heart of Christ. The believer must be ever prepared to defend the faith and give the answer for his hope in Jesus Christ.

Summary

This book was written to challenge the local church to place a heavy emphasis on training new members. The objective of the writer was to demonstrate through biblical scripture that ineffective preparation to present or represent Jesus Christ will have negative results for the preservation of Scripture and for the work of evangelism.

The writer expounds on the biblical evidence that preparation is essential before practice is engaged. The focus of this material directs the reader to be conscious of the necessity to equip and educate new members within the local church with basic biblical information that is pertinent to Christianity before they pursue the work of evangelism.

These five lessons are essential to learning the basics of being a Christian before attempting to do the work of evangelism:

- "Saved Solid" provides answers to the basic questions relating to salvation.
- "Soul Maintenance Plan" addresses the reason why spiritual immaturity within the local church fosters an environment for undeveloped disciples.
- "Spiritual Gifts" prescribes biblical applications and principles designed to assist

the believer in discovering his or her spiritual gift.

- "Sowing Seeds of Salvation" defines evangelism and explains why it is necessary. This lesson also gives techniques for the evangelism approach.

- "The Stewardship Lifestyle" describes how every previous lesson comes under stewardship, which is a total way of life based on gratitude to God.

Notes

1. Phan, Katherine T. "'Lost' Christians Greatest Crisis in American Church, says Author." *The Christian Post*. 9 May 2008. christianpost.com.
2. Phan, Katherine T. "'Lost' Christians Greatest Crisis in American Church, says Author." *The Christian Post*. 9 May 2008. christianpost.com.
3. Chua, Edmond. "Most Christians Cannot Explain Their Faith, Says Apologist." *The Christian Post*. 3 June 2010. christianpost.com.
4. McKnight, Tim. "5 Reasons We Don't Make Disciples." Anderson University College of Christian Studies. 6 Nov. 2014. http://auministry.com/5-reasons-disciples/.
5. MacDonald, James. "Unafraid Witness." *Vertical Church*. David Cook, 2012. p. 240—1.
6. Putman, Jim, and Avery T. Willis, Jr. *Real Life Discipleship Training Manual*. Colorado Springs: NavPress, 2010. Kindle edition.

7. Chan, Francis. *Multiply: Disciples Making Disciples*. Colorado Springs: David Cook, 2012. p. 9.

8. Ibid.

9. Ibid.

10. "Atheists and Agnostics Take Aim at Christians." *Barna*. The Barna Group. 11 June 2007. barna.org.

11. "'Nones' on the Rise." *Pew Forum on Religion & Public Life*. Pew Research Center. 9 Oct. 2012. pewforum.org.

12. "Ignosticism." *Atheism*. Wikia Inc. 7 March 2016. http://atheism.wikia.com/wiki/Ignosticism.

13. Wedell, Sherry A. *Forming Intentional Disciples: The Path to Knowing and Following Jesus*. Huntington, IN: Our Sunday Visitor, 2012. p. 17.

14. Barna, George. *Evangelism That Works*. Ventura, CA: Regal Books-Gospel Light, 1995. p. 22.

15. Douglass, Randy. "Closing the Back Door: The Need for Christian Education." *Dr. Norman L. Geisler*. 21 Oct. 2009. normangeisler.com.

16. Ibid.

17. Ibid.

18. Stevens, R. Paul, and Phil Collins. *The Equipping Pastor: A Systems Approach to Congregational Leadership*. Alban Institute, 1998. p. 2.

19. Phillips, John. *Exploring Acts*. Neptune, NJ: Moody Press, First Loizeaux Brothers, 1991. p. 61.

20. Barclay, William. *Daily Study Bible Series New Testament*. Rev. ed. Philadelphia: Westminster Press.

21. Idleman, Shane. "Can a Christian Lose Their Salvation?" *The Christian Post*. 14 May 2015. christianpost.com.

22. Kierkegaard, Sören. *Purity of Heart Is to Will One Thing*. Feather Trail Press, 2009.

23. Commentary by the Obama Administration

About the Author

The Reverend Dr. Oscar Terrance Moses is the second child of the late Oscar Moses and Rosetta Moses-Hill and the fifth generation to preach the gospel. He serves as the 17th Pastor of the Mt. Hermon Missionary Baptist Church, where his grandfather, the late Reverend Joseph A. Allen, served as pastor for 41 years.

Dr. Moses is a graduate of Mendel Catholic Preparatory High School of Chicago. He earned his Bachelor of Science Degree in Criminal Justice with a minor in Religious Studies from Southern Illinois University in Carbondale. On June 6, 2000, he received his Master of Arts in Theological Studies from McCormick Theological Seminary. On May 21, 2001, he received a Certificate of Completion for one extended unit of level one CPE by the Association for Clinical Pastoral Education, Inc. at Advocate South Suburban Hospital. Dr. Moses is a Mckissick Carter Fellow graduate of the United Theological Seminary, where he earned his Doctor of Ministry Degree in 2014. His dissertation was focused on *Preaching That Challenges Congregations to Transform Community Hopelessness to Hope and Beyond.*

Dr. Moses married his helpmeet, Jacqueline Marie, on July 27, 1996. She has earned a master's degree in Special Education from Saint Xavier University in Chicago as well as a doctoral degree in Educational Psychology from National Lewis University in Skokie, Illinois.

Dr. Moses has a passion for soul-winning. His commitment to teaching the Word of God has inspired the development of W.A.R. (**W**ord of God **A**pplied **R**ightly) Bible Study.

Dr. Moses is the President and CEO of Exodus Unlimited. The mission of Exodus Unlimited is to glorify our Lord and Savior, Jesus Christ, through community empowerment. On January 17, 2007, the University of Chicago Hospital recognized Exodus Unlimited during the Dr. Martin Luther King Jr. Awards Ceremony for providing After School Care to youth within the Auburn Gresham Community. The After School Care Program was created to reduce educational apathy, gang activity, and low reading scores within the community.

Dr. Moses serves as Moderator for the Christian Unity Baptist District Association. He is the Chairman of Evangelism for the Illinois National Baptist State Convention and the former Coordinator for the Evangelical Board Tent Revival for the National Baptist Convention of America, Inc. Dr. Moses is currently an adjunct professor at Trinity Christian College in Palos, Illinois, teaching "Christian Worldview." Dr. Moses is a member of Omega Psi Phi Inc. Fraternity.

Dr. Moses is a Bible-believing, God-trusting, and God-fearing servant of the Lord. His favorite scripture is: "Trust in the Lord with all thine heart; and lean not unto thine own understanding. In all thy ways acknowledge him, and he shall direct thy paths" (Proverbs 3:5-6 KJV). It is evident that God is truly directing his path as he continues to serve Him in spirit and in truth.

About Sermon To Book

![sermontobook.com logo]

SermonToBook.com began with a simple belief: that sermons should be touching lives, *not* collecting dust. That's why we turn sermons into high-quality books that are accessible to people all over the globe.

Turning your sermon series into a book exposes more people to God's Word, better equips you for counseling, accelerates future sermon prep, adds credibility to your ministry, and even helps make ends meet during tight times.

John 21:25 tells us that the world itself couldn't contain the books that would be written about the work of Jesus Christ. Our mission is to try anyway. Because, in Heaven, there will no longer be a need for sermons or books. Our time is now.

If God so leads you, we'd love to work with you on your sermon or sermon series.

Visit www.sermontobook.com to learn more.

www.ingramcontent.com/pod-product-compliance
Lightning Source LLC
Chambersburg PA
CBHW061820040426
42447CB00012B/2742